Famous First Facts

About Negroes

Famous First Facts

About Negroes

Romeo B. Garrett

ARNO PRESS

A NEW YORK TIMES COMPANY

NEW YORK ■ 1972

To
My Wife
Naomi S. Garrett

Contents

Famous First Facts

About Negroes

PREFACE

In the present work I have endeavored to amass many of the famous facts about American Negroes from their earliest beginnings in Africa down to the present time. It is not always easy to determine the "first" in a particular area. An effort has been made to include only those "firsts" for which there is substantial documentation. Further research into published and unpublished works may disclose additional data.

For convenience in use, the main entries have been catalogued in alphabetical arrangement, with many cross-references. A subject/name index is included.

As additional "first facts" about Negroes are brought to light, the author will appreciate having them called to his attention, with the hope of enlarging this body of information in subsequent editions of *Famous First Facts About Negroes*.

Without the research of Carter G. Woodson, Charles H. Wesley, W. E. B. Du Bois, Benjamin Quarles, John Hope Franklin, William M. Brewer, Joseph Nathan Kane, Henry A. Ploski, Roscoe Brown, Russell Adams, and numerous others who have contributed significant writings to the field, it would not have been possible for me to write this book.

To the library staffs of Bradley University and the Peoria Public Library I owe more than I can ever repay for their invaluable assistance in arranging interlibrary loans and in permitting me the fullest use of all their facilities. I am profoundly grateful to Mrs. Dorothy Porter, Director of the Moorland Foundation Collection at Howard University, for supplying me with priceless information on the Negro.

I am grateful to Bradley University for its research grant, which aided me in making this study. My thanks also go to Mrs. Mary Chelikas for her very careful checking and most helpful suggestions. The dedication of the work to my wife expresses inadequately my profound gratitude to her for her sacrifices and enthusiastic support of my efforts in writing.

Bradley University   *Romeo B. Garrett*
Peoria, Illinois
January, 1972

Abolitionism

The first formal abolitionist document in U.S. history was signed in 1688—the Germantown (Pa.) Mennonite Antislavery Resolution.

The first abolitionist society was the Society for the Relief of Free Negroes Unlawfully Held in Bondage. It was formed on April 14, 1775, in Philadelphia, Pennsylvania. The first president was John Baldwin. In 1787, the organization was incorporated as the Pennsylvania Society for Promoting the Abolition of Slavery and for the Relief of Free Negroes Unlawfully Held in Bondage and for Improving the Conditions of the African Race.

◆

The first and only Emancipation Proclamation was issued by Abraham Lincoln on January 1, 1863, after a preliminary document with similar content had been issued on September 22, 1862. The proclamation provided that all persons held as slaves in the states of Arkansas, Texas, Louisiana, Mississippi, Alabama, Florida, South Carolina, North Carolina, and Virginia "are, and henceforward shall be forever free." Exempted from this proclamation were several parishes (counties) in Louisiana and the city of New Orleans, all of which were in control of the Union forces; and the 48 counties of Virginia that had formed the separate state of West Virginia. Lincoln did not free the slaves held in states loyal to the Union or those in the border states of Kentucky, Missouri, and Maryland.

Actors

The first world-famous American Negro actor was Ira Aldridge. He was born in Maryland in 1807. By the time he had grown to manhood, America was not yet ready to appreciate a Negro in a Shakespearean role; Aldridge migrated to Europe. After

1

studying briefly at the University of Glasgow in Scotland, Aldridge went to London in 1825, where he appeared in the melodrama *Surinam, or A Slave's Revenge.* When he finally appeared in London's Theatre Royal in 1833, his portrayal of Othello was acclaimed by the critics as brilliant. During the 1850's, Aldridge was regarded as one of the two or three greatest actors in the world. He was honored and decorated by the King of Sweden, the King of Prussia, the Emperor of Austria, and the Czar of Russia.

Aldridge died in Lodz, Poland, on August 7, 1867. He is honored by a tablet housed in the New Memorial Theatre in Stratford-on-Avon, England.

◆

Charles Gilpin was the first modern American Negro to establish himself as a serious actor of first quality. In 1920, he appeared in the title role of O'Neill's *The Emperor Jones.* In 1921, Gilpin was awarded the coveted NAACP Spingarn Medal for his performance in the O'Neill play.

◆

The first major all-Negro motion picture, *Hallelujah,* was produced by King Vidor in 1929. Although well received, it did not open the doors for the general participation of Negroes as actors in Hollywood.

◆

The first Negro ever to win an Oscar was Hattie McDaniel, who received the Motion Picture Academy's highest award in 1940 as the best supporting actress in *Gone With the Wind.*

Miss McDaniel was born on June 10, 1898, in Wichita, Kansas, and moved to Denver, Colorado, as a child. After singing on Denver radio as an amateur for some time, she entered vaudeville professionally and, by 1924, was a headliner on the Pantages circuit.

In 1931, Miss McDaniel moved to Hollywood, where she appeared in such movies as *Judge Priest, The Little Colonel, Showboat, Saratoga,* and *Nothing Sacred.* Her portrayal of a mammy figure in *Gone With the Wind* was regarded as superb.

In addition to her movie roles, she had abundant success on radio, particularly as *Hi-Hat Hattie* and *Beulah.* Hattie McDaniel died on October 26, 1952.

◆

Sidney Poitier was the first Negro actor to have his hands and feet imprinted in the cement of Grauman's Chinese Theater in Hollywood.

Poitier was born on February 20, 1924, in Miami, Florida, but moved to the Bahamas with his family at a very early age. At fifteen he returned to Miami, and thence to New York. In New York, he auditioned for the American Negro Theatre but was turned down by director Frederick O'Neal. After working diligently to improve his diction, Poitier was accepted in the theater group and received acting lessons in exchange for performing backstage chores. In 1965, he won the Oscar as best actor for his portrayal of an itinerant construction worker in *Lilies of the Field.* Among Poitier's other films are *No Way Out; Cry, the Beloved Country; Red Ball Express; Go, Man, Go; Blackboard Jungle; Porgy and Bess; In the Heat of the Night; To Sir, with Love; Guess Who's Coming to Dinner?; Edge of the City; Goodbye My Lady; A Raisin in the Sun; The Defiant Ones; Band of Angels; Something of Value;* and *For Love of Ivy,* the latter based on a story written by Poitier.

See also Drama; Film; Radio; Television.

African Methodist Episcopal Church

The first African Methodist Episcopal Church was the Bethel African Methodist Episcopal Church, founded in 1787 by Richard Allen, a Negro, at Sixty and Lombard streets in Philadelphia, Pennsylvania.

It was a pew incident that sparked the origin of this church. On a winter Sunday morning in 1787, as Richard Allen and Absolam Jones—who had founded the Free African Society seven months earlier—were kneeling in prayer at St. George's Episcopal Church in Philadelphia, a trustee advanced upon them, pulled Jones up, and said that the blacks must go to the rear of the gallery. When Jones' request that they be permitted to finish their prayers was denied, the two Negro leaders walked out of St. George's, never to return. The forty Negroes who sat with them in the segregated balcony also walked out.

They followed Allen to a blacksmith's shop where they knelt in prayer. The one-room shack where this first congregation of

Mother Bethel Church worshiped God still smelled of horses, and Allen used the smith's anvil for his rostrum. Allen increased his congregation and purchased a building, which was dedicated by Bishop Francis Asbury as the Bethel Methodist Episcopal Church, whose membership was limited to Negroes. What the Negroes wanted was summed up by Bishop Asbury while in Baltimore in 1795: "The Africans of this town desire a church, which, in temporals, shall be altogether under their own direction."

In 1816, Allen called together others from four states to found the African Methodist Episcopal denomination. He was elected its first bishop.

Today a sturdy three-story $68,000 building stands as a shrine to AME's throughout the Americas and Africa on the same spot where the unknown blacksmith once wielded his hammer. Since 1816, over nine thousand AME churches like Mother Bethel have sprung up. Sixteen bishops preside over a membership totaling 1,650,000. Ten AME colleges flourish. The AME's believe that God is our Father, Christ our Redeemer, and man our Brother. This was the idea in Richard Allen's mind when he founded Mother Bethel; it remains the theme of the AME church today.

African Methodist Episcopal Zion Church

The first African Methodist Episcopal Zion church was established by James Varick, a shoemaker.

In 1796, a group of Negroes led by Varick withdrew from the John Street Methodist Church in New York City because of its policy of separating Negro and white members of the congregation, and held its first meeting in a carpenter's shop in lower Manhattan. The first church, to which they gave the name African Methodist Episcopal Zion (AMEZ), was built in 1800 at the corner of Church and Leonard streets. It was incorporated in 1801 and rebuilt in 1820 to accommodate the greatly increased number of worshipers. The first annual conference met in 1821, and in that year, Varick was elected their first bishop.

From the first handful of New York Negroes meeting in the carpenter's shop in 1796, the AME Zion Church has grown to nearly a million members in the United States, Africa, South America, and the West Indies.

Afro-American Unity

The first leader of the Organization of Afro-American Unity was Malcolm X. With the O.A.A.U., he hoped not only to unite black people in the United States but all nonwhites throughout the Western Hemisphere. The philosophy of black unity is now in operation.

Born Malcolm Little in Omaha, Nebraska, on May 19, 1925, he was the son of a Baptist preacher who was an avid supporter of Marcus Garvey's United Negro Improvement Association. At an early age, Malcolm moved to Lansing, Michigan, with his parents, both of whom were tragically lost to him in childhood. (His father was murdered by whites in 1931, and his mother was committed to a mental institution.) Without parental support, Malcolm began an almost predictable behavioral pattern of delinquency and crime, but showed better than average talents before dropping out of school after the eighth grade. He moved to New York, working for a time as a waiter at Small's Paradise in Harlem. In Harlem, he drifted into the underworld of "numbers," bootlegging, dope, prostitution, and confidence games. Soon he turned to burglary, and was sentenced to a ten-year prison term in 1946.

It was in the state prison at Charlestown, Massachusetts, that he learned of the Black Muslim sect headed by Elijah Muhammad, and was quickly converted to its utopian and strongly racist point of view. Paroled from prison in 1952, he soon became an outspoken spokesman for the Muslim doctrines, accepting the basic argument that evil was an inherent characteristic of the "white man's Christian world."

Malcolm made several provocative and inflammatory statements while addressing predominantly white civic groups and college campus audiences. He branded white people as blue-eyed devils. When in 1963, he characterized the Kennedy assassination as a case of "chickens coming home to roost," he was suspended from the Black Muslim movement by Elijah Muhammad, and in the same year formed his own protest group, the Organization of Afro-American Unity.

Malcolm traveled the length and breadth of the nation with a message of black manhood and independence, and made two voyages to the Middle East and Africa. The effect of these travels was to increase his optimism regarding brotherhood between blacks and whites the world over. In his *Autobiography* he wrote: "I tried in every speech I made to clarify my new position regarding white people—I don't speak against the sincere, well-meaning good white people. I have learned that there are some. I have learned that not all white people are racists. I am speaking against and my fight is against the white *racists*."

On February 21, 1965, Malcolm was assassinated in the Audubon Ballroom in New York City. His death was headlined around the world.

Airline Stewardesses

Ruth Carol Taylor, a graduate nurse of Ithaca, New York, was the first Negro airline stewardess in the history of commercial aviation in the United States. Her employment represented the culmination of several months of negotiations that had been under way between the New York State Commission Against Discrimination and the major airlines operating in New York. She was hired by Mohawk Airlines, and made her first flight on February 11, 1958, from Ithaca to New York City.

Almanacs

The first Negro to publish an almanac in the United States was Benjamin Banneker, a freeborn Maryland Negro. His book was designed for use by farmers and contained the usual weather predictions, tips to farmers, tide tables, data on future eclipses, useful medicinal products, and, occasionally, lofty editorials. In one such editorial, Banneker urged the appointment of a secretary for peace in the national cabinet. This almanac was the first scientific book written by an American Negro and it appeared annually for more than a decade.

Banneker got the idea of publishing an almanac for farmers of his own region in Maryland as a result of his continuing study of astronomy. He set to work, and the first almanac appeared in 1792, when he was nearly sixty. The book was eagerly sought by farmers of four states. Banneker presented a handwritten copy to Thomas Jefferson, with whom he frequently corresponded. Jefferson later sent it to Condorcet, secretary of the French Academy of Sciences.

A member of John Adams' cabinet had one of Banneker's

almanacs published in Baltimore. This patron, James McHenry, said that the almanac was begun and finished without outside assistance except the loan of books "so that whatever merit is attached to his present performance, is exclusively and peculiarly his own." The publishers declared that the almanac met the approbation of several of the distinguished astronomers of America.

Ambassadors

Edward R. Dudley was the first Negro to serve in Liberia with the rank of ambassador. He was appointed in 1948 by President Harry S Truman.

Dudley was born in South Boston, Virginia, and March 11, 1891. He earned a law degree at St. John's Law School.

The first Negro to be made officially an ambassador was Clifton R. Wharton. President John F. Kennedy appointed him Ambassador to Norway in 1961.

Born in Baltimore on May 11, 1899, Wharton received his LL.B. from Boston University in 1920, the same year he was admitted to the Massachusets bar. In 1923, he won his LL.M. from Boston University.

Wharton entered the U.S. Foreign Service in 1925, functioning as third secretary to Monrovia, Liberia. Over the next three decades, he held such posts as consul at Tananarive (Malagasy Republic); consul and first secretary to Lisbon (Portugal); and Minister to Rumania. In this last post, he became the first Negro diplomat to head a U.S. delegation to a European country. Wharton resigned from his Norway post in 1964, after thirty-nine years in diplomatic service.

Mrs. Patricia Roberts Harris, an assistant law professor at Howard University, became the first black woman in the United States to be named an ambassador. President Lyndon B. Johnson appointed Mrs. Harris ambassador to Luxembourg in 1965. She was born in Mattoon, Illinois. Her undergraduate degree was received from Howard University in 1945. After completing post-graduate work at the University of Chicago and at American

University, she earned her doctorate in jurisprudence from George Washington University Law School in 1960. She is a Phi Beta Kappa and a member of numerous professional and civic organizations.

See also Diplomatic Corps.

Armed Forces

The first person to die for the cause of American freedom was a Negro—Crispus Attucks. On the night of March 5, 1770, the intimidating presence of British soldiers in Boston excited the indignation of the people of Massachusetts. One group, later described by John Adams as "a motley rabble of saucy boys, Negroes and mulattoes, Irish Teagues and outlandish Jack Tars," decided to protest the action. Led by Crispus Attucks, a runaway slave from Framingham, Massachusetts, they rushed into King Street, shouting, "The way to get rid of these soldiers is to attack the main guard." They were fired upon by several men of Captain Preston's company. Attucks was the first to die, thus becoming the first martyr to American liberty and the inaugurator of the revolution that was destined to take from the crown of George III its brightest star. By the sacrifice of his life, Attucks awoke that fiery hatred of British oppression that culminated in the declaration of American independence.

Attucks' prominent role in the Boston Massacre owed much to John Adams, who, as counsel defending the British soldiers, chose to make him the chief target. Adams informed the trial jury that it was Attucks who "appears to have undertaken to be the hero of the night; and lead this army with banners, to form them in the first place in Dock square and march them up to King Street with clubs." It was Attucks "whose very looks was enough to terrify any person," who "had hardiness enough to fall in upon them, and with one hand took hold of a bayonet, and with the other knocked the man down." It was Attucks "to whose mad behavior, in all probability, the dreadful carnage of that night is chiefly to be ascribed."

Attucks' one impulsive attack wrote his name undyingly in the annals of American history, for patriots did not allow the Boston Massacre to be forgotten. March 5 was called Crispus Attucks Day and was duly observed each year in a public ceremony, which took on a ritualistic pattern. Bells would toll during the day, and at night lighted transparencies depicted the soldiers and their victims, giving a substance of sorts to the "discontented ghosts, with hollow groans," summoned to solemnize the occasion. The highlight of the evening was a stirring address by a leading citizen which, as the contemporary historian David Ramsay observed, "administered fuel to the fire of liberty, and kept it burning with an incessant flame."

Years later Adams got back into the good graces of New England and the colonies by saying what the people had felt all along. Of March 5, he said, "On that night the foundation of American independence was laid."

◆

The first blood of the Civil War was shed by a Negro, Nicholas Biddle. On April 18, 1861, Biddle and a group of volunteers from Pottsville, Indiana, were hurrying to Washington to answer President Abraham Lincoln's call for soldiers to protect the nation's capital from the gathering Southern troops. While marching through the streets of Baltimore with his company, Biddle was struck in the face with a brick, and from him poured the first blood of the Civil War. Other volunteers were hit, but Biddle was the first. Blood still oozed from his wound when the company arrived in Washington. Ninety years after this incident, the citizens of Pottsville erected a plaque, "In memory of the First Defenders and Nicholas Biddle of Pottsville, First man to shed blood in the Civil War, April 18, 1861. Erected by citizens of Pottsville, April 18, 1951."

◆

The first Negro to become a captain in the U.S. Navy was Robert Smalls. During the early days of the Civil War, Smalls took a Confederate steamer, the *Planter,* and ran it out of the Charleston harbor. He delivered it to the Union Navy saying, "I thought the *Planter* might be of some use to Uncle Abe." President Lincoln turned the ship into a gunboat and made Smalls a captain in 1863. From 1883 to 1887 he served as congressman from South Carolina. A school in that state now bears his name.

◆

The first Negro to be commissioned chaplain in the U.S. Army was Henry McNeal Turner, pastor of the Israel African Methodist Episcopal Church in Washington, D.C. He was commissioned U.S. Chaplain by President Abraham Lincoln in early 1863. After passing through thirteen bloody battles and many skirmishes, Turner was mustered out with his regiment in the fall of 1865, but was recommissioned U.S. Chaplain in the regular army by President Andrew Johnson within ten days. He was detailed to work in the Freedmen's Bureau and was assigned to Georgia. After serving a short time as an officer of the bureau and finding that the church needed his services infinitely more than the government, Turner sent in his resignation and devoted his time and talents to the ministry. Later he became a member of the Georgia legislature, a bishop of the AME Church, chancellor of Morris Brown College, founder of several denominational periodicals, compiler of a catechism and a hymnbook, and recipient of an honorary degree (LL.D.) from the University of Pennsylvania.

◆

The first Negro to win the Congressional Medal of Honor was Sergeant William H. Carney, Company C, 54th Massachusetts Colored Infantry. Carney was born in New Bedford, Massachusetts. In 1863, he received his medal for his heroism in the Battle of Fort Wagner, during the Civil War, when, against tremendous odds, he held his regimental colors high and swore: "The old flag never touched the ground, boys." During this battle, Carney was wounded severely twice. His deed was remembered in a poem:

THE OLD FLAG NEVER TOUCHED THE GROUND

"The Old Flag never touched the ground!" 'twas thus brave
    Carney spoke,
A Negro soldier: words renowned, that Honor will invoke
Upon the records of the Race whose heroes many are,
Records that Time cannot efface, and Hate can never mar.
Those words were stamped with Carney's blood upon our
    Country's scroll,
And though dislike, deep as a flood, against his Race may
    roll,
It cannot dim, nor wash away, its crimson-written fame
Which History wrote on Wagner's day without a tinge of
    shame.

Not only Carney did she view, when with immortal pen
She stood to write the honors due one thousand Colored men
Who laughed at death, who felt no fear, and followed Colonel
Shaw
Where none but heroes dared to go, with cheer and loud
hurrah.

July the eighteenth, of the year eighteen-and-sixty-three,
To Negroes always will be dear, as any one could be,
For bloody cost of honors won, for loss of noble life,
For valor that no risk would shun in fiercest battle strife.

◆

The first Negro in the navy to receive the Congressional
Medal of Honor was Robert Blake, an ex-slave. He distinguished
himself during the Civil War while serving as a powder boy on
board the *U.S.S. Marblehead* in an engagement with the Confederates in the Stono River, off Legareville, South Carolina, on December 25, 1863. The commander of the *Marblehead,* Richard W.
Meade, Jr., reported that Blake "excited my admiration by the cool
and brave manner in which he served the rifle gun." The action of
the Union warship caused the Confederates to abandon their island
position, leaving a caisson behind.

◆

The first Negro to become a field officer in the U.S. Army was
Martin R. Delaney. He received his commission on February 5,
1865, and was ordered to report to Charleston, South Carolina. He
was assigned to assist in recruiting and organizing black troops at
Charleston. By the end of the war he had attained the rank of
major.

Delaney was a free-born native of Charleston, West Virginia,
but spent his youth in Pennsylvania, where he was taken to be
educated. He received his medical and scientific training at Harvard University and practiced medicine in Chicago and Canada. He
helped Frederick Douglass to edit *The North Star* from 1847 to
1849. For a short time, Delaney published his views in his own
newspaper called *The Mystery.* He also published two major books,
*The Condition, Elevation, Emigration and Destiny of the Colored
People of the United States Politically Considered* (1852), and
Principia of Ethnology: The Origins of Race and Color (1879).

After the war, Delaney worked with the Freedmen's Bureau for three years. Later he became a customs inspector in Charleston, South Carolina, and then a trial justice in the same city. He died on January 24, 1885.

◆

The first Negro to enter the U.S. Military Academy at West Point was James W. Smith of South Carolina, who was admitted to West Point in 1870. Smith did not graduate, and after almost four years at West Point, he left and became supervisor of cadets at South Carolina Agricultural Institute in Orangeburg—now the South Carolina State College.

◆

The first Negro to enter the U.S. Naval Academy at Annapolis was James H. Conyers. This took place in 1872.

◆

The first Negro to graduate from West Point was Henry O. Flipper of Thomasville, Georgia. Following his graduation on June 15, 1877, he was assigned to the 10th Cavalry Regiment. Four years later, Flipper was separated from the army and began an engineering career which carried him to Arizona, Mexico, and eventually Venezuela.

◆

The first Negro graduate of West Point to achieve distinction in the military was Colonel Charles Young. He graduated from West Point in 1889. Upon graduation, Young was assigned to the 10th Cavalry. His career in active service took him to Mexico, Haiti, Liberia, and Cuba, where he rode with Theodore Roosevelt and his Rough Riders in the famous charge up San Juan Hill. Young served as professor of military science and tactics at Wilberforce University, military attaché to Haiti, a member of the 2nd Division's general staff, military attaché to Liberia, and a staff officer in the office of the Army's Chief of Staff. With the outbreak of World War I, Colonel Young expected to be given an assignment overseas. Military doctors examined him only to announce that his health was too poor at that time for active duty. Angered by this, Young mounted his favorite horse at Chillicothe and rode the five hundred miles back to Washington, D.C., as proof of his fitness for service. Instead of being retired for "reasons of health," he was assigned to the Ohio National Guard. Colonel Young returned to Liberia in 1919, and three years later, while conferring with native chiefs, he became seriously ill and died at a hospital in Lagos, Nigeria.

◆

The first four Negro soldiers in the Spanish-American War to receive the Congressional Medal of Honor were: Private Dennis Bell (Troop H, 10th U.S. Cavalry; born, Washington, D.C.), Private Fitz Lee (Troop M, 10th U.S. Cavalry; born Dinwiddie County, Virginia), Private William H. Thompkins (Troop G, 10th U.S. Cavalry; born Paterson, New Jersey), and Private George Wanton (Troop M, 10th U.S. Cavalry; born, Paterson, New Jersey). They received their medals on June 23, 1899, for bravery at Tayabacoa, Cuba.

◆

The first army camp for training Negro officers was established on June 15, 1917, at Fort Des Moines, Iowa, and was known as the 17th Provisional Training Regiment. On October 15, 1917, the first commissions were granted, 106 Negroes being commissioned as second lieutenants.

◆

The first *Croix de Guerre* awarded to a Negro in the American army was given to Private Henry Johnson, 369th Infantry, 93rd Division, on May 24, 1918, with the following citation:

> While he was on double sentry duty at night, his post was attacked by twelve Germans. He shot one and seriously wounded two others with his bayonet. Even though he had been three times wounded at the beginning of the action by revolver bullets and grenades, he went to the assistance of his wounded comrade, who was about to be carried off by the enemy, and continued to combat until he put the Germans to flight. It was a splendid example of courage and energy.

◆

The first Negro general in American history was Benjamin O. Davis, Sr. He won his promotion to brigadier general in October, 1940, during the final years of a dedicated army career.

Davis was born on June 1, 1887, in Washington, D.C. He was educated in the public schools and briefly attended Howard University. But when the Spanish-American War broke out, he left school and entered the service as a temporary first lieutenant in the 8th U.S. Infantry. In a career that spanned fifty years, Davis saw combat in three wars, serving both in the infantry and the horse cavalry. He also served as military attaché to Liberia and as assistant to the army's inspector general. After retirement, Davis lived in Washington, D.C., until his death in November, 1970.

◆

The first Negro ever to win the Navy Cross was Dorie Miller, a messman aboard the *U.S.S. Arizona,* who, on December 7, 1941, during the Pearl Harbor attack, manned a machine gun and brought down four Japanese planes. The award was made by Admiral Chester W. Nimitz, the commander-in-chief of the Pacific fleet.

Miller's role at Pearl Harbor helped dramatize Jim Crow in the Navy, where Negroes were relegated to messman's jobs only. Steps were taken under the direction of the Secretary of the Navy to admit Negroes to all ranks, and today U.S. ships at sea have Negroes serving in many positions previously barred to them.

Dorie Miller went back to sea after receiving his Navy Cross, and little more than a year and a half after Pearl Harbor he lost his life when the aircraft carrier *Liscome Bay* was sunk in the bitter fighting off Tarawa in the Pacific. Miller's memory is enshrined in the records of the Navy Department and in Negro history as the man whose heroism touched off a campaign to eliminate the color line in the navy and give Negro sailors a chance to defend their country not with mops but with guns.

◆

The first army aviator to down an Axis airplane was First Lieutenant Charles Hall, a Negro, of Brazil, Indiana. In a Warhawk, as part of a fighter squadron escorting bombers, Hall shot down a German Focke-Wulf 190 over Sicily on July 2, 1943. Lieutenant Colonel Benjamin O. Davis, Jr., of Washington, D.C., was squadron commander. Hall was awarded the Distinguished Flying Cross and credited with the all-Negro 99th Fighter Squadron's first aerial victory when he destroyed the German plane in aerial combat.

◆

The first two Negroes chosen to attend the Naval War College in Newport, Rhode Island, were Lieutenant Commander George I. Thompson and Commander Samuel L. Gravely. The date of their selection was March 24, 1963. Thompson graduated from UCLA as an English major. Gravely, the highest ranking Negro in the regular navy, was educated at Virginia Union University and, late in 1944, became the first Negro to be graduated from a midshipman's school.

◆

The first Negro flier of the U.S. Naval Reserve was Jesse Leroy Brown of Hattisburg, Mississippi, who was commissioned ensign on April 15, 1949. He crashed on December 4, 1950, near the Changjin Reservoir in Korea, thus becoming the first Negro flier killed in action in Korea.

◆

The first Negro to graduate from the U.S. Naval Academy was Wesley A. Brown. He graduated in June, 1949.

◆

The first Negro soldier in the Korean war and the first since the Spanish-American War to receive the Congressional Medal of Honor was Pfc. William Thompson, Company M, 24th Infantry. Born in Brooklyn, New York, Thompson lost his life on August 6, 1950, after fighting off the enemy singlehanded during a withdrawal operation. The medal was awarded in June, 1951.

◆

On October 27, 1954, Benjamin O. Davis, Jr., paralleled his father's career when he became the first Negro general in the history of the air force. On this date he became General Davis—the highest ranking Negro in the history of America.

◆

The first Negro to head the National Veterans Organization was W. Robert Ming, a lawyer in Chicago. Ming was elected to the position in 1957.

◆

The first Negro sentry to guard the Tomb of the Unknown Soldier in Arlington National Cemetery was Fred Moore. Moore was posted at the tomb in 1961.

◆

The first Negro to be assigned the command of a Navy warship was Lt. Commander Samuel L. Gravely. In 1962, Gravely took over the command of the destroyer escort *U.S.S. Flagout,* whose assignment was to patrol the western Pacific Ocean.

◆

The first Negro soldier in Vietnam to receive the Congressional Medal of Honor was Milton Lee Olive III, Company B, 503rd Infantry, 173rd Airborne Brigade. Olive, who was born in Chicago, saved the lives of his fellow soldiers by falling on a live grenade and absorbing the shock of its blast with his own body. He was cited for conspicuous gallantry by President Lyndon B. Johnson at the White House on April 21, 1966, at which time the medal was presented to his parents. Olive died a few weeks before his nineteenth birthday.

◆

The first Negro astronaut was Major Robert Lawrence of Chicago, Illinois. An eleven-year veteran of the air force, Lawrence began his career in the Bradley University ROTC. After graduating with a B.S. degree in chemistry, he went into flight training. In 1961, after duty in West Germany, Lawrence returned to earn his Ph.D. in nuclear chemistry at Ohio State University. While at Ohio State, Lawrence became interested in the space program. He applied for the program in 1965, and was announced in June, 1967, as being one of sixteen persons chosen for astronaut training out of five hundred applicants. He had accumulated more than 2,500 hours of flying time.

Lawrence was killed in December 1967, in the crash of an F-104 Starfighter at Edwards Air Force Base in California.

◆

The first Negro in Marine Corps history to receive the Congressional Medal of Honor was Pfc. James Anderson of Compton, California. The nation's highest award for heroism was awarded posthumously on August 21, 1968, to Anderson, who gave his life to save his comrades in Vietnam.

◆

The first Negro woman to achieve the rank of colonel in the air force was Ruth Lucas of Alabama. She joined the old WAAC in 1942, and was promoted to full colonel on November 25, 1968.

◆

The first two Negro cadets to win top honors at West Point were Keith B. Holmes of Gallup, New Mexico, and Malcolm N. Colbert of Sacramento, California.

Holmes was chosen "Best New Cadet" from the original 1,375-man cadet class of 1974. Malcolm Colbert won the Superintendent's Award and Trophy for the outstanding third classman (sophomore) at Camp Brucker, the academy's two-month training camp for second-year cadets.

◆

The first Negro admiral in U.S. naval history is Captain Samuel L. Gravely, Jr. Admiral Gravely was 48 at the time of his promotion.

Selection of Gravely was made by the Navy's Flag Selection Board which met on April 13, 1971, to pick 50 officers for promotion to rear admiral. The names were sent to President Nixon, who nominated them and relayed them to the Senate for confirmation. Admiral Gravely's promotion was confirmed on May 15, 1971.

A veteran of three wars, Gravely saw services in World War II, aboard a submarine chaser and in the Korean War on the cruiser *Toledo*.

Art

The first Negro portrait painter to win recognition in America was Joshua Johnston of Baltimore, Maryland. Johnston was listed among "Free Housholders of Color" in the Baltimore Directory of 1796. His work still hangs in Baltimore museums.

◆

The first Negro to win acclaim as an important American regional painter was Robert Bannister. He was born in Nova Scotia in 1828, studied in Boston, and then moved to Providence, Rhode Island, where he remained until his death in 1901. Some of his better-known landscapes include: *Sabin Point, Narragansett Bay* and *After the Storm.*

The first great Negro artist to live solely from his art was Henry O. Tanner. He was born in Pittsburgh in 1859, the son of an African Methodist minister. Tanner studied at the Academy of Fine Arts in Philadelphia and became a photographer in Atlanta. Afterward he taught at Clark University in Atlanta. Due to race prejudice in America, he went to live in Paris. As a painter, Tanner directed his attention largely to religious life, as evidenced by the names of his paintings. His works include *The Raising of Lazarus, Disciples at Emmaus, The Annunciation, Judas, Nicodemus, Daniel in the Lions' Den, The Disciples,* and *The Wise and the Foolish Virgins.* He is regarded as the most distinguished Negro in the field of art.

Australian Citizenship

The first American Negro believed to be approved for Australian citizenship by the immigration authorities under the relaxed rules for admitting non-Caucasians as permanent settlers was Barnard Byers. He was approved in December, 1970. Byers has been an instructor in French at the private Trinity Grammar School in Melbourne for four years. He believes he is the first Negro to teach in an Australian school.

Banks

The first depositor in the first savings bank in the United States was a Negro. Curtis Roberts, who was a servant in the home of Condy Raquet, one of the founders of the Philadelphia Saving Fund Society, is the man whose first silver dollar started that bank on the road to deposits of more than $200,000,000.

The first bank organized and managed entirely by Negroes was the Savings Bank of the Grand Fountain United Order of True Reformers. The bank was chartered on March 2, 1888, and began operations on April 3, 1889, with a paid-up capital of $4,000. It was begun by a fraternal order founded by William W. Browne.

◆

The first bank for Negroes privately operated by Negroes and independent of fraternal connections was the Capital Savings Bank of Washington, D.C., which was organized on October 17, 1888, with a capital of $6,000. Among the prominent promoters and directors were Robert H. Terrell, Whitfield McKinley, W. S. Montgomery, John Pierre, R. R. Wilder, and Henry Baker. John R. Lynch once served as its president.

◆

The first woman bank president in America and the only one of the Negro race was Mrs. Maggie L. Walker, who founded the Saint Luke Penny Savings Bank in Richmond, Virginia, which was incorporated on July 28, 1903. The bank had a paid-in capital of $25,000.

◆

The first Negro to be elevated to a major executive post in a New York City bank was Richard B. Cardwell. He was named assistant vice-president of the Empire City Savings Bank in 1965.

◆

The first Negro banker in the nation to head a formerly all-white bank was Norman A. Simon, a native of New Orleans. Simon was elected president of Guaranty Bank & Trust Company in Chicago, at a board of directors meeting on March 28, 1967.

Baptist Church

The first Negro Baptist Church in America and indeed the first Negro church was established in 1773, by a Mr. Palmer at Silver Bluff, South Carolina. Palmer was one of a group of slaves owned by George Galphin, who became a patron of the little congregation and permitted David George to be ordained for this special work after having previously allowed George Liele to preach there. The congregation continued to worship here in comparative peace until the latter part of 1778, when the vicissitudes of war eventually led the flock across the Savannah River to Augusta, Georgia, twelve miles away. This church is known today as the Springfield Baptist Church.

◆

The Reverend Dr. Thomas Kilgore, Jr., became the first Negro to take over as head of the American Baptist Convention in its sixty-two-year history in May, 1969.

Dr. Kilgore had led the union organization and voter registration of tobacco workers in Winston-Salem, North Carolina, in 1943–44. He supervised the New York office of the Southern Christian Leadership Conference from 1959 to 1963, helped organize the March on Washington in 1963, and is a leader in the National Association for the Advancement of Colored People.

Baseball

The first Negro professional baseball team was the Cuban Giants, organized in New York City in 1885. S. K. Govern was manager. The players received expenses and weekly salaries according to positions: pitchers and catchers, $18; infielders, $15; outfielders, $12.

◆

The first Negro major-league baseball player was Jackie Robinson of the Brooklyn Dodgers, who played in an exhibition game on April 11, 1947, against the New York Yankees. He played first base in the exhibition game and throughout that season.

Robinson was born in Georgia and was reared and educated in California. In 1949, he won the National League's Most Valuable Player Award. He played with the Brooklyn Dodgers for ten years and was elected to the Baseball Hall of Fame in 1962. Robinson retired from baseball in 1956, and assumed the vice-presidency of the Chock Full O' Nuts Corporation.

◆

The first Negro umpire in organized baseball was Emett Littleton Ashford of the Class C Southwestern International League, who was authorized as a substitute umpire on February 20, 1952, by league president Les Powers. Ashford became the first Negro umpire in the major leagues in 1966.

Basketball

The first Negro basketball team to be enshrined in the Basketball Hall of Fame was the Renaissance basketball team. This team was founded in October, 1922, by Robert L. Douglass in Harlem in New York City.

The first Negro National Basketball Association player was Charles Henry Cooper, an all-star player who played his first game for the Boston Celtics on November 1, 1950, in Fort Wayne, Indiana, against the Fort Wayne Pistons.

The first Negro to serve as coach of a team in the National Basketball Association was Bill Russell. He retired in 1969 as player-coach of the Boston Celtics.

Russell was born on February 12, 1934, in Monroe, Louisiana. The family moved to Detroit when he was nine. Two years later, after his mother died, the Russells continued on to Oakland. There, at McClyronds High School, Russell proved to be an awkward but determined basketball player; he eventually received a scholarship to the University of San Francisco. Here, he became the most publicized athlete on the West Coast. Over the next two years, Russell's fame spread across the nation as he led his team to sixty consecutive victories and two straight NCAA titles.

Named Sportsman of the Year in 1968 by *Sports Illustrated* magazine, Russell led the Celtics to eleven National Basketball Association championships in thirteen seasons.

The first Negro ever to serve as head coach in the NCAA (National Collegiate Athletic Association) University Division was

Will Robinson, who became head basketball coach at Illinois State University in the fall of 1970.

Robinson holds a B.S. in education (1937) from West Virginia State College and a master's in education (1938) from the University of Michigan. He has done additional work at Wayne State University.

Robinson has spent 38 of his 58 years as coach at the YMCA and high school levels in Pittsburgh, Chicago, and Detroit. He has won eighty-five percent of their games.

Beauty Contests

The first Miss Black America was Saundra Williams, a young Philadelphian who wears her hair natural, does African dances and helped lead a student strike at her college in the spring of '67.

On September 8, 1968, the 5-foot, 4-inch 125-pound Miss Williams edged out seven other black beauties in a contest held in the Ritz Carlton Hotel in Atlantic City, New Jersey. At this time she was 19 years old.

"This is better than being Miss America," she said after the pageant. "Miss America does not represent us because there has never been a black girl in the pageant. With my title, I can show black women that they too are beautiful. . . . There is a need to keep saying this over and over because for so long none of us believed it. But now we're finally coming around."

When Miss Williams was a sociology major at Maryland State College, she was informed that Negroes were not allowed to eat in a restaurant in Princess Anne, Maryland, home of the predominantly Negro college. So she helped to organize a group of students called the Black Awareness Movement, which staged a silent protest march against the white business community. As a consequence the restaurant was integrated.

The first black entrant in the Miss America contest was Miss Cheryl Andreanne Brown of Decorrah, Iowa, who entered the contest at Atlantic City, New Jersey, in 1970 after being chosen Miss Iowa.

The first black woman to win the title of "Miss World" was Jennifer Josephine Hosten, who represented the island of Grenada, West Indies, in the contest held at Albert Hall in London, England, on December 3, 1970. Miss Hosten is an airline stewardess with British West Indies Airways.

The first black woman to win the 1970 title in the pageant's twenty-year history is the youngest daughter in a family of five. Her father is an attorney in Grenada.

"Black Is Beautiful"

The saying "black is beautiful" was first articulated by Dr. John Rock, a Boston doctor and lawyer, who was, in 1858, the first Negro admitted to practice before the United States Supreme Court.

"Black Power"

The term "black power" was first used by Richard Wright, who authored a book in 1954 entitled *Black Power*. Wright, a Mississippi Negro, was writing about blacks on the Gold Coast of Africa. By this term he meant the power of blacks to control their own destiny.

Representative Adam Clayton Powell used the term "black power" at a Chicago rally in May, 1965, and elaborated on it in a Howard University commencement address in May, 1966.

The term "Black Power" was popularized by Stokely Carmichael on a Mississippi night in June, 1966, during the march on the state capitol, which was led by James Meredith. Shouted again and again by Carmichael, then the fiery chairman of the Student Nonviolent Coordinating Committee, the phrase was picked up and hurled back by an angry crowd, and finally was amplified across the nation by the press, radio, and television. The term was further popularized by Carmichael, who with Roosevelt University Professor Charles V. Hamilton wrote a book entitled *Black Power*.

Blind

The first school for the Negro blind was the State School for the Blind and Deaf, opened in Raleigh, North Carolina, on January 4, 1869, with twenty-six pupils.

Bowling

The first Negro to be elected to the board of directors of the American Bowling Congress was William H. Hall, Sr., an active member in various community organizations in Chicago, and a topflight bowler. He was elected in April, 1970. A retired Chicago policeman, Hall has been active in Chicago circles as a league bowler and top official. In February, 1970, he qualified in the Chicago North section of the *Sun-Times* Beat-The-Champion bowling contest but was unable to reach the finals.

"I never dreamed I would be nominated for this office—there are many others who have been active in bowling for many years," said Hall upon his election.

Boxing

The first American heavyweight contender for the heavyweight championship of the world was a Virginia slave, Tom Molineaux, who won his freedom with his fists by defeating the champion of a neighboring plantation. The boxing world in Molineaux' day was England, so he journeyed there around 1809, thrashed eight British boxers, and earned a crack at the current champion Tom Cribb. The Cribb-Molineaux match, considered the first international title bout, was fought on December 18, 1810, before several thousand spectators. Molineaux lost the fight. A return match was granted on September 28, 1811, which resulted in another defeat for Molineaux. He died in Galway, Ireland, in 1818, at the age of thirty-four.

◆

The first Negro heavyweight champion of the world was Jack Johnson, regarded by many as the greatest heavyweight champion of all time. On December 26, 1908, he defeated Tommy Burnes at Sydney, Australia, in fourteen rounds, thereby technically winning the championship. The actual title was earned on July 4, 1910, when Johnson defeated James Jackson (Jim) Jeffries in fifteen rounds at Reno, Nevada. Johnson lost his title on April 5, 1915, at Havana, Cuba, to Jess Willard in twenty-six rounds. In 1946,

Johnson died in an automobile crash in North Carolina. When the Boxing Hall of Fame opened in 1954, his was the first name ratified.

◆

The first and only fighter ever to hold three titles at one time was a Negro, Henry Armstrong, who accomplished this feat on August 17, 1938, when he added the lightweight championship to the featherweight and welterweight titles which he had won earlier.

◆

The first fighter to hold the heavyweight championship longer than a decade was Joe Louis. Louis was born in a sharecropper's shack in Chambers County, Alabama, in 1914. He held the championship from 1937 to 1949—11 years, 8 months, and seven days—and defended it more times than any other champion. His 25 title fights were more than the combined total of the eight champions who preceded him.

Cabinet

See Presidents and the Negro.

Catholic Church

See Roman Catholic Church.

Christian Methodist Episcopal Church

The Christian Methodist Episcopal Church, known until 1956 as the Colored Methodist Episcopal Church, had its beginnings after the Civil War when some 250,000 segregated Negroes belonging to the Methodist Episcopal (ME) Church South appealed to the General Conference for the right to form their own church. In 1870, the request was granted. In December of that same year, the first General Conference of the CME Church was held in Jackson, Tennessee, where two Negro bishops—Harry Miles and Richard H. Vanderhorst—were elected. Since then the two churches have cooperated in many ways, primarily in the field of education. The CME Church operates three colleges, several secondary schools, and a seminary.

Church

The Negro church was the first distinctly Negro-American social institution. It was by no means a Christian church at first but rather a mere adaptation of those rites of fetish, which in America are termed animism or voodooism. Association and missionary effort soon gave these rites a veneer of Christianity and gradually, after nearly two centuries, the church became Christian, with a simple Calvinistic creed but with many of the old customs still clinging to the services. The first Negro denominational church in the United States was the Baptist church established in 1733 at Silver Bluff, South Carolina.

◆

The first Negro minister of an all-white church was the Reverend Lemuel Haynes. After soldiering in the Revolutionary War, Haynes was ordained by the Congregational Church in 1785, and for over forty years served congregations in Massachusetts, Connecticut, Vermont, and upstate New York. This man became one of the most famous ministers of his day.

See also specific demoninations.

Church of God in Christ

The Church of God in Christ was founded by Reverend Charles Harrison Mason in Lexington, Mississippi. Because they "spoke in tongues," danced the holy dance, and believed that men could not be saved without holiness, a small band of Baptists was ejected from the little Baptist church in Arkansas in 1895. The leader of the ejected group, Dr. Mason, organized a new sect and called it the Church of God in Christ because such a name "would not depart from the scriptures and at the same time distinguish the true followers from the false." Today the church has a membership of nearly one million. Mason also founded Saints Junior College in Lexington, Mississippi.

Bishop Mason, the founder and senior Bishop, died at an advanced age in December, 1961.

Cities

The man who is considered to have made the first permanent settlement in Chicago was Jean Baptiste Point du Sable, a Negro. The estimated date of his settlement is 1779. He was also the first to see the commercial advantages of the city's location.

Prior to his settlement in Chicago, this stalwart pioneer lived in Peoria for at least six years, during which time he became outstanding in business, agriculture, and politics.

Of du Sable, St. Clair Drake, a prominent Negro scholar, has written:

> At "the place of evil smell," du Sable erected a frontier establishment consisting of a large wooden homestead, bake-house, smokehouse, poultry house, and dairy; a workshop and a horse mill; a barn and two stables. Here the Pottawato-mie came to trade; and the English and French exploring and fighting for dominance in the back-country, stopped to rest and replenish their stores. Reclaimed from the prairie and wrested from the wilderness, this solitary frontier settle-ment became the seed-bed of skyscrapers and factories. Its trading post was the progenitor of the wheat-pit and its workshop the prototype for factories and mills. The canoes and pirogues that stopped here foreshadowed the commerce of after-years.

Today a plaque marks the spot in Chicago where du Sable built his home; a high school in the city is named in his honor; and an organization known as the National du Sable Memorial Society exists to revere his memory.

◆

The first Negro director of a major city's planning department in the United States was Charles Clayborne Allen. He was appoint-ed by Mayor Richard C. Hatcher on July 5, 1968, and assumed his position as Director of Department of Planning, City of Gary, Indiana, on July 29, 1968.

Civil Rights

The United States Supreme Court's first significant civil rights decision was in the *Amistad* case in 1841. The case is a historical event in that the Court ruled that human beings could not be held as chattel—thereby dooming slavery in the U.S. The case grew out of the American capture of the Spanish slave ship *Amistad,* which was manned by slaves who had revolted. The young African leader Cinque, a prince, and his followers were defended before the Supreme Court by former President John Quincy Adams, who based his argument on the inherent right of every human being to be free. The Supreme Court ruled in favor of the slaves, and declared them free to return to Africa.

The *Armistad* papers are a group of documents relating to a maze of arguments and claims in the case of the slaves who revolted. These papers will be permanently housed at Dillard University, a predominantly black institution in New Orleans, Louisiana. The priceless papers, a collection of more than three million documents, letters, and creative works, will be housed in the William Alexander Library until the construction of the National Amistad Research Center.

◆

The first civil rights act was the Civil Rights Act of 1866. It was designed to protect the freedman from the Black Codes and other repressive legislation. This measure conferred citizenship upon Negroes and set the stage for the more inclusive Fourteenth Amendment. It was passed by Congress over the veto of President Andrew Johnson.

Congregational Church

The first Negro Congregational Church was the Dixwell Avenue Congregational Church. This church had its beginnings in 1820, when a white man, Simeon S. Jocelyn, gathered in New Haven twenty-four black persons to offer them religious instruction —principally the teachings of the Bible. He met much abuse and received many threats from whites, but his congregation grew until, in 1829, they became a regular Congregational church.

In 1836, the church called to its pastorate the celebrated clergyman, Reverend J. W. C. Pennington. Pennington, who was born a slave, became one of the best educated men of his day, and the degree of Doctor of Divinity had been conferred upon him by the University of Heidelberg in Germany.

Congress

The first Negro to be allowed in the House of Representatives as well as the first Negro minister to deliver a sermon in the Chambers of the House was Reverend Henry Highland Garnet, pastor of the Fifteenth Street Presbyterian Church in Washington, D.C. Dr. Garnet's sermon was in commemoration of the adoption of the Thirteenth Amendment. Previously Negroes were forbidden to enter the grounds. His sermon was delivered on Sunday, February 12, 1865, to a crowded chamber, and is considered one of the masterpieces of Negro eloquence.

◆

The first Negro elected to Congress was John Willis Menard of New Orleans, Louisiana. During the Civil War, he came to Washington and was appointed a clerk in the Bureau of Emigration of the Interior Department. This appointment marked the first time a Negro had held a clerkship in government service.

In 1865, at the termination of the Civil War, Menard moved to New Orleans, where he was first appointed inspector of customs and later became street commissioner. In 1868, Menard was nominated and elected on the Republican ticket to the 40th Congress to fill the unexpired term of James Mann, who had died on August 28, 1868. A bizarre three-way contest for the seat developed when Caleb S. Hunt, a Democrat, challenged Menard's election, while Simon Jones, a Republican, contested the right of the deceased James Mann to have held the seat. The House of Representatives decided against all three claimants, and the seat remained vacant until Lionel A. Sheldon was seated in the 41st Congress on March 4, 1869. But all three men were given $2,500, the pay they would have received if they had been seated.

Since Menard was never seated, the distinction of being the first Negro to serve in Congress cannot be granted to him. However, he may be credited with another important "first." During the course of the debate on the question of whom to seat, a motion was passed to allow each contestant fifteen minutes to state his case. Menard was the only one to avail himself of this privilege and thereby became the first Negro to speak on the floor of the House of Representatives.

◆

The first Negro to serve in the U.S. Senate was Hiram Rhodes Revels, who was born of free parents in Fayetteville, North Carolina, on September 27, 1827. He was educated at a Quaker school in Indiana, and attended Knox College in Galesburg, Illinois. He was ordained in the African Methodist Episcopal ministry in 1845. Following his ordination he worked among Negro settlers in the Northwest Territory and in the border states of Kentucky and Missouri before settling in Baltimore, Maryland. There he served as a church pastor and school principal.

During the Civil War, Revels helped organize a pair of Negro regiments in Maryland, and, in 1863, he went to St. Louis to establish a freedmen school and carry on his work as a recruiter. For a year he served as chaplain of a Mississippi regiment before accepting the post as provost marshall of Vicksburg. While in this part of the country, he was also active in organizing a number of Negro churches.

Revels settled in Natchez, Mississippi, in 1866, and became pastor of the Zion Chapel African Methodist Episcopal Church, beginning the career that was to take him to the United States Senate. He was elected as alderman of Natchez in 1868, and to the state senate in 1870. When the state legislators of Mississippi convened in January, 1870, preacher Revels was called on to open the session with a prayer. His prayer was impressive and did much to lead to his election as United States Senator. Mississippi had no representative in the Senate after Jefferson Davis resigned at the beginning of the Civil War. When Mississippi reentered the Union in 1870, Revels was elected as a compromise candidate.

On March 17, 1870, Revels gave his maiden speech in the Senate. The occasion of Revels' speech was the readmission of Georgia into the Union. Referring to his race, he spoke in behalf of civil liberties:

> They appeal to you and to me to see that they receive that protection which alone will enable them to pursue their daily avocations and enjoy the liberties of citizenship on the same footing with their white neighbors and friends. I maintain that the past record of my race is a true index of the feelings which today animate them. They aim not to elevate themselves by sacrificing one single interest of their white fellow-citizens. They ask but the rights which are theirs by God's universal law, and which are the logical sequence of the conditions in which the legislative enactments of this nation have placed them.

In the galleries, Negro and white men and women were listening intently. There were more Negro men than white in the galleries that day; in the gallery reserved for ladies, there were as many Negro women as white. The Diplomatic Gallery was filled with the relatives of Senators who had not been able to gain admission elsewhere. Revels continued:

> I rise to plead for protection of the defenseless race which now send their delegation to the seat of Government to sue for that which this Congress alone can secure to them. And here let me say further, that the people of the North owe to the colored race a deep obligation which it is no easy matter to fulfill. When the Federal armies were thinned by death and disaster, from what source did our nation in its seeming death throes gain additional and new-found power? It was the able sons of the South that valiantly rushed to the rescue, and but for their intrepidity and ardent daring many a northern fireside would miss today paternal counsel or a brother's love.
>
> Many of my race, the representatives of these men on the field of battle, sleep today in the countless graves of the South. If those quiet resting-places of our honored dead could speak today, I think that this question of immediate and ample protection for the loyal people of Georgia would lose its legal technicalities, and we would cease to hesitate in our provisions for their instant relief.

Revels' year in the Senate was marked by a quiet but determined fight to improve race relations in the South, obtain Negro rights, and rebuild the shattered economy of Mississippi. Some of the measures that he advocated have a startlingly contemporary sound. He called for integration of District of Columbia schools in 1871—a change that did not take place until after the 1954 Supreme Court decision. Also, he called for abolishing segregation on railroads and other common carriers.

Revels' term came to a close on March 3, 1871. He did not run for reelection. Alcorn College for Negroes was established near Rodney, Mississippi, and Revels became its first president. He was appointed by Governor Alcorn, who was to replace him in the U.S. Senate. In June, 1876, Revels went to New Orleans to edit the *Southwestern Advocate,* an organ of the General Conference of his church. After serving two terms as president of Alcorn, Revels returned to religious work and made his home in Holly Springs, Mississippi. He became district superintendent of his church conference and died while attending a church conference at Aberdeen, Mississippi, on January 16, 1901.

The first Negro ever to serve in the House of Representatives was Joseph Hayne Rainey. Born on June 21, 1832, in Georgetown, South Carolina, Rainey received a limited education and then became a barber. In 1870, he was elected to the 41st Congress from the first district of South Carolina to fill the vacancy caused by the resignation—and subsequent condemnation by the House for improper conduct—of Frank Wittmore. Rainey took office on December 12, 1870, and served until 1879.

In Congress, Rainey served on the Committee on Freedmen's Affairs and worked for legislation to enforce the Fourteenth Amendment. He was an ardent supporter of the 1870 Ku Klux Klan Act, and in his own right presented numerous petitions for the passage of a civil rights bill that would guarantee Negroes their full constitutional rights, including equal access to public accommodations. In fighting for this latter provision, Rainey staged what was one of the first sit-ins when he refused to leave the dining room of a Suffolk, Virginia, hotel and was forcibly ejected by the management. Other legislation that Rainey advocated included a bill to establish a steamship line between the United States and Haiti and legislation to protect the rights of the Chinese in California. During his years in Congress, Rainey made another important "first." He was the first Negro to preside over the House of Representatives during a debate. He died on August 1, 1887, in Georgetown, South Carolina.

The first Negro ever to serve in Congress from the state of Georgia was Jefferson Franklin Long. He was born a slave near Knoxville, Georgia, in March, 1836. A self-educated man, Long moved to Macon, Georgia, while a young man and obtained work with a merchant tailor there. Eventually he saved enough money to open a shop of his own. In 1869, he won the Republican nomination for representative from the fourth district of Georgia to fill the vacancy caused by the House's declaring Samuel F. Gove not entitled to the seat. Long served from December 22, 1870, to March 21, 1894.

The first Negro congressman ever elected from the state of Florida was Josiah Walls, who was born in Winchester, Virginia, on December 20, 1842. His education was very limited, as was that of most Negroes of his day. In 1870, Walls was elected a Republican congressman-at-large to the 42nd Congress; he was reelected to the 43rd and 44th Congresses. His last election was contested, and on April 19, 1876, he was forced to yield his seat to Jesse J. Finley.

During his tenure in Congress, Walls served ably on the Committee on the Militia. For humanitarian reasons he strongly backed the position that the United States should lend military support to the insurgent Cubans who were then revolting against Spain. Spain had not only brought African slaves to the island to work on plantations but also had enslaved and brutally mistreated the native Indian population.

After the close of his congressional career, Walls returned to his farm in Florida. A severe frost brought him close to financial ruin, so he accepted the post of superintendent of a farm on the campus of Tallahassee State College. He died in Tallahassee on May 5, 1909.

◆

The first Negro congressman from the state of Mississippi was John Roy Lynch, who was born a slave in Concordia Parish, Louisiana, on September 10, 1847. In 1863, he was taken to Natchez, Mississippi, where after emancipation he took up the profession of photography. By attending night school he managed to obtain a good education.

Lynch was elected to the House of Representatives on three separate occasions—1873, 1875, and 1881. During his years in Congress, Lynch's greatest contribution was his speech on behalf of civil rights, which was delivered during the second session of the 43rd Congress. This speech was considered by many Negro scholars to be a masterpiece of eloquence. A contemporary wrote: "There are not a dozen men in the House on either side who can excel Lynch either in the graces of oratory or in the literary finish of their discourse. He has a pleasant voice, clear and penetrating, an easy mode of gesture, and is entirely free from any blemish of extravagance, either in the matter or style of his delivery."

At the close of his congressional career, Lynch's interest in politics did not terminate. In 1884, a unique tribute was paid him in that he became the first Negro to preside over the Republican

National Convention, which met in Chicago. In 1889, Lynch served under President Benjamin Harrison as Fourth Auditor of the United States Treasury, and in 1898, during the Spanish-American War, President McKinley named him U.S. Paymaster with the rank of major.

Lynch retired to law practice in 1911, and during his later years, he wrote two books: *The Facts of the Reconstruction* and *Some Historical Errors of James Ford Rhodes.* Lynch died in Chicago, on November 2, 1939.

The first Negro senator to serve a full term in the United States Senate was Blanche K. Bruce, who was born a slave in Farmville, Prince Edward County, Virginia, on March 1, 1841. Bruce received his early formal education in Missouri, the state to which his parents had moved while he was quite young. He later studied for two years at Oberlin College in Ohio.

In 1868, Bruce made Mississippi his permanent home by settling in the town of Floreyville. Prior to his election to the U.S. Senate, Bruce held several positions of trust and honor in Mississippi. He had been Sheriff, Tax Collector, Commissioner of the Levees Board, and County Superintendent of Education. Moreover, he had served as Sergeant-at-Arms of the first state senate after the Reconstruction period, and Commissioner of Elections in a county that was reputed to be the most lawless in the state.

In 1874, Bruce was elected as a Republican to the U.S. Senate from Mississippi; he served until March 3, 1881. He was assigned to the Committee on Manufacturers, the Committee on Education and Labor, and later to the Committee on Pensions and the Committee on the Improvement of the Mississippi River and its Tributaries. Bruce's maiden speech in the Senate was delivered shortly after he took his seat during the special session called by President Grant. The speech was a vigorous protest against the proposed removal of the troops from the South—Mississippi in particular—where the military authorities were still in control. The speech made a profound impression on the Senate and clearly indicated the manly stand that Bruce was preparing to take against the injustices practiced against Negro citizens in both North and South. Bruce became an outstanding defender of the rights of minority groups, including those of the Chinese and the American

Indians. He also investigated alleged election frauds and worked for the improvement of navigation on the Mississippi River in the hope of increasing interstate and foreign commerce. Like Revels, Bruce supported legislation aimed at eliminating reprisals against those who had opposed Negro emancipation.

The Republican party met in convention in Chicago in June, 1880, and Blanche K. Bruce was proposed for the vice-presidency. He received eleven votes on the first ballot and was the first of his race to be considered for nomination for the vice-presidency by a major political party.

After Bruce completed his term in the Senate, he served as Register of the Treasury, having been appointed to this office by President Garfield. In 1889, during the administration of President Benjamin Harrison, Bruce was appointed Recorder of Deeds when the office was operated under a system of fees which netted the officeholder from twelve to fifteen thousand dollars a year. President McKinley called him a second time to the office of Register of the Treasury, in which position he remained until his death in 1898, in Washington, D.C.

The first Negro to serve the state of North Carolina as congressman was John A. Hyman, who was born a slave near Warrenton, North Carolina, on July 23, 1840. He was sold and sent to Alabama, where he remained until after the Civil War. In 1875, Hyman, who was self-educated, was elected as a Republican to the 44th Congress from the second district of North Carolina. He served on the Committee on Manufacturers during his term in Congress.

At the close of his congressional career, Hyman returned to agricultural pursuits. In 1877, he was appointed Special Deputy Collector of Internal Revenue for the fourth district of North Carolina, and served there until 1878. He died in Washington, D.C., on September 14, 1891.

The first Negro to serve as congressman from Louisiana was Charles Edmund Nash, who was born on May 23, 1844, in Opelousas, Louisiana. He received a limited education and was working as a bricklayer when, in 1863, he enlisted in the Union Army. He lost a leg during the storming of Fort Blakely in

Alabama—the last infantry battle of the Civil War—and was honorably discharged with the rank of sergeant major. He was then appointed night inspector of customs in Louisiana.

Nash was elected as a Republican from the sixth district of Louisiana to the 44th Congress in 1874 and served on the Committee on Education and Labor. He consistently preached brotherhood. "We are not enemies but brethren," he told blacks and whites. "This is our joint inheritance. Over brothers' graves, let brothers' quarrels die."

At the close of his congressional career, Nash returned to Louisiana and accepted an appointment as postmaster at Washington, Louisiana, where he served from February 15 to May 1, 1882. He died in New Orleans, on June 21, 1913.

◆

The first Negro to serve as congressman from Virginia was John Mercer Langston, who was born a slave in Louisa, Virginia, on December 14, 1829. After the death of his father and owner, he was emancipated and sent to Ohio where he lived with a friend of his father's and attended school. In 1849, Langston graduated from the literary department of Oberlin College; he graduated from the theological department in 1852. He studied law in Elyria, Ohio, was admitted to the bar in 1854, and began his law practice in Oberlin.

Langston had a long and illustrious career. In 1855, he became the first Negro elected to public office in the United States when he won the post of township clerk in Brownhelm, Ohio. During the Civil War, he was a recruiter for the famed Negro regiments of the 54th and 55th Massachusetts and the 5th Ohio. He was a member of the council of Oberlin from 1865 to 1867, and a member of the city board of education in 1867 and 1868; he was appointed inspector general of the Bureau of Freedmen, Refugees, and Abandoned Lands in 1868; from 1869 to 1876 he was dean of the law department of Howard University; he was appointed and commissioned by President Grant a member of the Board of Health of the District of Columbia in 1871; he was appointed by President Hayes as minister resident and consul general to Haiti and chargé d'affaires to Santo Domingo; and in 1872, he was elected vice-president and acting president of Howard University.

In 1890, Langston successfully contested the election of Edward C. Venable to the 51st Congress and served from September

23, 1890, to March 3, 1891, as a Republican from the fourth district of Virginia.

Defeated in his bid for a second term, Langston nonetheless remained interested in politics. In 1894, he wrote an autobiography, *From the Virginia Plantation to the National Capital.* He died in Washington, D.C., on November 15, 1897.

◆

The first Negroes who went to Congress following the Civil War were commonly thought to be ignorant and helpless; but House Speaker James G. Blaine, who knew most of them, said the reverse was true: "They were as a rule studious, earnest, ambitious men, whose public conduct would be honorable to any race."

◆

The first Negro congressman to be elected from a northern state and from the state of Illinois was Oscar DePriest, who was born in Florence, Alabama, on March 9, 1871. In 1878, he moved to Salina, Kansas, where he attended school. He took up the trade of painter and decorator, and in 1889, he moved to Chicago, where he became a real estate broker. His political ambitions were largely thwarted until, in 1915, he became Chicago's first Negro alderman —a position he held until 1917. In 1928, DePriest was elected as a Republican to the 71st Congress from the first district of Illinois; he was reelected to the 72nd and 73rd Congresses. In Congress he served on the committees on Enrolled Bills, Indian Affairs, Invalid Pensions, and Post Office and Post Roads. As a member of Congress he fought against the color line in the House of Representatives restaurant. Although DePriest served in Congress only three terms and was unseated by the swing of Negro votes to President Franklin Roosevelt and the Democrats' New Deal, he established himself as one of the truly outstanding men in U.S. politics. He died in Chicago on May 12, 1951.

◆

The first Negro Democrat to be elected to Congress was Arthur Mitchell, who was born on a farm near Lafayette, Alabama, on December 22, 1883. He attended public school in Alabama and then went on to Tuskegee Institute, Columbia University, and Harvard. Young Mitchell literally sat at the feet of his idol, Booker T. Washington, in the early years of his life. Like Washington, Mitchell left Tuskegee and founded a rural school, Armstrong Argicultural School, in West Butler, Alabama. He studied law and was admitted to the bar in 1927, and he began practice in Washington, D.C. In 1929, he moved to Chicago, where he continued his practice of law and also engaged in real estate. He served as an alternate delegate to the Democratic National Convention in 1926, a delegate-at-large to the convention in 1940, and was the first Negro to address a national convention.

In 1934, he defeated Negro Republican Oscar DePriest for his seat in Congress and served from the 74th to the 77th Congress. His service in Congress was on the Committee on Post Office and Public Roads. In Congress, Mitchell became an ardent advocate of civil rights legislation, but his most significant victory in this field came not in Congress but in the courts. In 1937, he had brought suit against the Chicago & Rock Island Railroad for forcing him to leave his first-class accommodations while en route to Hot Springs, Arkansas. Mitchell argued his own case before the Supreme Court in 1941, and won a decision which declared that Negroes who purchase first-class tickets may not be denied Pullman berths or any of the accommodations that go with first-class tickets.

While in Congress, Mitchell introduced three bills; an anti-lynch bill; a bill to prohibit the use of photographs as a means of identification in connection with civil service appointments; and a bill to create an industrial commission on Negro affairs.

Declining renomination in 1942, Mitchell settled on his estate near Petersburg, Virginia, until his death in 1968.

◆

The first Negro congressman from New York was Adam Clayton Powell, Jr., who was born on November 29, 1908, in New Haven, Connecticut. He attended public school in New York City, and graduated from Colgate University in Hamilton, New York, in 1930; he received an M.A. degree from Columbia University in 1932, and won an honorary doctor of divinity from Shaw University for his successful pastorate of the Abyssinian Baptist Church in Harlem. In 1941, he became New York's first city councilman. He also edited and published a newspaper, *The People's Voice,* which he called "the largest Negro tabloid in the world."

In 1945, Powell was elected as a Democrat to Congress from the 18th district of New York; he was reelected to each succeeding

Congress until 1970, when he was defeated in the Democratic primary by Charles Rangel, also a Negro. Because of his intense interest in civil rights legislation, Powell has been called "Mr. Civil Rights." He fought hard for the abolition of discriminatory practices at U.S. military installations around the world and sought—through the controversial Powell amendment—to deny federal funds to any project where discrimination existed. This amendment eventually became part of the Flanagan School Lunch Bill, making Powell the first Negro congressman since Reconstruction to have had legislation passed by both houses. He likewise sponsored legislation advocating federal aid to education, a minimum wage scale, and greater benefits for the hard-core unemployed. He called attention to the long-standing discriminatory practices on Capitol Hill itself. It was Powell who first demanded that a Negro journalist be allowed to sit in the Senate and House press galleries and it was he who introduced the first anti-Jim Crow transportation legislation as well as the first bill to prohibit segregation in the armed forces.

In 1960, Powell, as senior member, became the chairman of the powerful House Education and Labor Committee. Under his leadership, a number of major bills have become law, including the Minimum Wage Act of 1961, the Manpower Development and Training Act, the National Defense Education Act, the Vocational Education Act, and the Juvenile Delinquency Act.

In 1967, Powell was barred from his seat in the 90th Congress for "gross misconduct." But in 1969 the Supreme Court found 7 to 1 that Powell had been unjustly deprived of his seat and hence should be allowed to reenter. In 1970, he lost in his bid for reelection to Congress. He continues to serve as pastor of Abyssinian Baptist Church in Harlem.

Though he has been controversial at times, it is the general consensus of opinion that Powell has been the most powerful Negro political figure in Harlem and in the nation for the past quarter of a century.

◆

The first Negro to head a congressional committee was Representative William L. Dawson (D. Ill.). He was named chairman of the House Committee on Government Operations in 1948. He also served as vice-chairman of the Democratic National Committee and was the first Negro to hold such a position in either major political party. Dawson died of pneumonia in Chicago's Veterans Research Hospital on November 9, 1970.

◆

The first Negro congressman from Michigan was Charles C. Diggs, who was born in Detroit, Michigan, on December 2, 1922, and attended the local schools. He also attended the University of Michigan at Ann Arbor from 1940 to 1942, and entered Fisk University in Nashville, Tennessee, in the fall of 1942. While still a student, Diggs joined the army as a private but soon was commissioned a second lieutenant. He was discharged in 1945, and in September of that year he enrolled in the Wayne State University School of Mortuary Science. At the same time, he was radio commentator on a program cosponsored by the House of Diggs, the family business, which has come to be the largest funeral home in Michigan.

Diggs began his political career in 1951, when he was elected to the state senate. He served with distinction until 1954, when he was elected as a Democrat to the 84th Congress. He has been reelected to each succeeding Congress. Diggs has been constantly on the lookout for discrimination in federally financed programs, and has also been active in promoting equal treatment in the armed forces; he has traveled to U.S. military installations all over the world, investigating the grievances of soldiers. He serves on the House Foreign Affairs and District of Columbia committees.

◆

The first Negro congressman from Pennsylvania was Robert Nelson Nix, who was born on August 9, 1905, in Orangeburg, South Carolina. He attended private schools in New York City, graduated from Lincoln University in Chester County, Pennsylvania, and from the University of Pennsylvania Law School in 1924. In 1925, he was admitted to the bar and practiced law in Philadelphia. Nix served as special deputy attorney general of the Pennsylvania State Department of Revenue and special assistant deputy attorney general of the Commonwealth of Pennsylvania from 1934 to 1938.

In 1958, he was elected to the 85th Congress to fill the vacancy caused by the resignation of Representative Earl Chudoff; he has served from May 20, 1958, to the present. Nix is now serving on the Foreign Affairs, Post Office, and Civil Service committees. A longtime supporter of the civil rights movement, Nix was one of the first congressmen to speak in support of the Montgomery bus boycott; he has continued to give his backing to the civil rights movement.

◆

The first Negro congressman from California was Augustus F. Hawkins, who was born in Shreveport, Louisiana, on August 31, 1907. He moved to California when he was eleven years old and attended the local schools. Graduating from UCLA with an A.B. in economics and from the Institute of Government at the University of California, he became active in juvenile delinquency prevention work in Los Angeles County. In 1934, he was elected to the state assembly, and for the next twenty-eight years he remained in the assembly, authoring or co-authoring over three hundred laws on the California statute books in the field of civil rights.

After his service in the state assembly, Hawkins was elected to Congress in 1963 to represent the 21st district of California. He has been elected to each succeeding Congress and is presently serving on the Committee on Education and Labor, a committee whose jurisdiction encompasses labor relations, health, welfare, and housing, in addition to education.

◆

The first Negro to be elected to the U.S. Senate in the twentieth century was Edward W. Brooke, who was born in Washington, D.C. He attended the local public schools and went on to graduate from Howard University. Returning from World War II, in which he had risen to the rank of captain, Brooke attended the Boston University Law School, compiling an outstanding academic record. After law school, he established himself as an attorney and also served as chairman of the Boston Finance Commission. In 1962, Brooke was elected Attorney General for the state of Massachusetts. He won the election to the U.S. Senate as a Republican over former Massachusetts Governor Endicott Peabody on November 8, 1966.

◆

The first Negro congressman from Missouri was William Clay, the firebrand of Negro demonstrations in St. Louis in 1968. While serving as a St. Louis alderman, he was a leader in the Negro demonstrations against alleged discrimination in hiring practices at the Jefferson Bank and Trust Company.

In 1968, at the age of thirty-six, Clay defeated his Negro Republican opponent, Curtis Crawford, a former assistant circuit attorney, 77,074 to 43,109, thus assuming the congressional seat occupied by Democrat Frank Karston, a white man who had announced his retirement.

◆

The first Negro woman to be elected to Congress was Mrs. Shirley Chisholm of Brooklyn, New York. Born of West Indian parents, Mrs. Chisholm received a master's degree from Columbia University. She is an effective orator, an ardent civil rights worker, and attracts support from a broad cross-section of her community, including the poorest welfare mothers. In 1968, Mrs. Chisholm, a Democrat, challenged nationally known James Farmer in a race for Congress to represent a newly created district in the Bedford-Stuyvesant section of Brooklyn. She pounded the pavements of her 12th district seeking help and then floored her opponent at the polls by a vote of 36,142 to 12,023.

Conventions

The first national Negro convention was held in Philadelphia from September 20 to September 24, 1830. Approximately forty delegates representing various Negro organizations of seven states including New York, Pennsylvania, Maryland, Delaware, and Virginia—met in the historic Bethel Methodist Church. Many delegates risked their lives to attend, for gangsters dogged their footsteps, and mobs were organized to break up the convention. The convention first met in secret sessions for five days, from September 15–20, and voted to hold open sessions, come what may. Bishop Richard Allen of the African Methodist Episcopal Church was elected president of the convention. Other leading figures were James Forten, Reverend Samuel E. Cornish, Reverend Peter Williams, William Hamilton, Philip A. Bell, Hezekiah Grice, John Vashon, John T. Hilton, and Reverend J. W. C. Pennington. These men represented various Negro groups, united to protect their rights and to render aid to their unfortunate brethren who had been driven into exile. The American Society of Free Persons of Colour, for Improving their Condition in the United States; for

Purchasing Lands; and for the Establishing of a Settlement in Upper Canada was organized by the convention with auxiliaries to be established in every community. Each auxiliary was to send five delegates to the annual convention.

With the principles of the Declaration of Independence as their guide, the convention called upon all free colored people to utilize all legal means at their command to raise their economic, educational, political, and social status, and fight against slavery. They took a determined stand against the American Colonization Society, regardless of the honest motives that might direct some of its members in their efforts to send Negroes back to Africa.

Postconvention meetings were held in the larger cities such as Baltimore, New York, Boston, Pittsburgh, and Washington. Members pledged support to the plans outlined by the convention leaders. Typical of the stand taken by the masses of the Negro people was the meeting held on January 25, 1831, resulting in an address setting forth the "Resolutions of the People of Color, and to the Citizens of New York, in answer to those of the New York Colonization Society:"

> Resolved . . . that we claim this country, the place of our birth, and not Africa, as our mother country; and all attempts to send us to Africa, we consider as gratuitous and uncalled for.

◆

The first Negro to attend a national political convention in the capacity of delegate was Frederick Douglass. He attended the National Loyalist Convention (a convention of radicals in Congress whose aim was equality for the Negro) in Philadelphia, Pennsylvania, on September 6, 1866. His stirring address on behalf of Negro suffrage, which received the official endorsement of the convention, laid the groundwork for the Fifteenth Amendment.

◆

The first national nominating convention held by a major political party which was presided over by a Negro met in the Exposition Building in Chicago, Illinois, on June 3, 1884. John R. Lynch, a Negro, three times congressman from Mississippi, was nominated for temporary chairman of the Republican party by Henry Cabot Lodge. The nomination was supported by Theodore Roosevelt and George William Curtis and was carried by a vote of 424 for Lynch to 384 for Powell Clayton.

Creole

The first appearance of the word *creole* is found in the archives of the St. Louis Cathedral in the Baptismal record, dated 1779, of a slave from Jamaica who was referred to as a *negre creole*. In a latter entry in these archives, a person at first designated as Marie, *mulatresse,* is referred to in the body of the record as *une creole.*

Dance

The rhumba was first performed among Cuban Negroes as a rural dance depicting simple farm chores. The conga and the newer mambo originated among the Congo Negroes of Cuba. The tango, too, had its origins among Latin American Negroes. The national dance of Brazil, the samba, is derived directly from the wedding dance of Angola, the Quizomba. The Charleston, the Black Bottom, and the cakewalk were first developed by Negroes in the United States. All these dances have their roots in black Africa.

The first Negro to dance for the Metropolitan Opera Company in New York was Janet Collins. Miss Collins was signed by an agent of the company in 1951, and made her debut in *Aida*. She was born in New Orleans of mixed Negro, French-Creole, and Indian ancestry.

The first Negro to join the world-famous New York City Ballet, which is the largest ballet company in this country, was Arthur Mitchell.

Mitchell was born in New York City March 27, 1934. After finishing grade school he entered the High School of Performing Arts, where he majored in modern dance. During his senior year he went to Paris to perform in the opera, *Four Saints in Three Acts.*

He joined the New York City Ballet in 1958. He has appeared in *Western Symphony, A Midsummer Night's Dream, Agon, Araede, Modern Jazz, Variants, Pan America, Creation of the*

World, the Unicorn, The Gargon and the Manticare, Piege de Lumière, The Nutcracker, The Figure in the Carpet, Afternoon of a Faun, Carmen Jones, Kiss Me Kate, and many others; Mitchell has danced with John Butler Co. and with William Dollar's Ballet Theatre Workshop; he has choreographed (with Rod Alexander) for Shinbone Alley and the Newport Jazz Festival; he has danced and choreographed at the Spoleto Festival of Two Worlds in 1960; and he has taught dance at the Katherine Dunham School, the Karel Shank Studio, the Melissa Hayden School, and the Jones-Hayward School Ballet in Washington.

◆

The first Negro dance company to tour the U.S.S.R. was the Alvin Ailey Dance Company.

Ailey studied dancing after graduating from high school, where he was a star athlete. With a short stint in college behind him, he formed his own dance group in 1961.

Ailey, a product of the Lester Horton Dance Theatre in Los Angeles, has been called in America and abroad the "greatest modern male dancer." After Horton's death, Ailey served as choreographer and artistic director of the company for several seasons before moving to New York.

◆

The first Negro choreographer at the Metropolitan Opera House was Katherine Dunham. She was in charge of the ballet for a new production of *Aida*, which opened the 1963–64 season. She is one of America's most creative dancers and choreographers.

Born in Chicago on June 22, 1910, Miss Dunham attended the University of Chicago, where she majored in anthropology. With the aid of a Rosenwald Fellowship, she traveled far afield in search of Afro-Caribbean and American Negro rituals, rhythms, and patterns of movement.

In 1940, she appeared in *Cabin in the Sky,* a musical for which she did some choreography. She later toured the United States and the major cities of the world with her own dance group for twenty years. In 1966, Miss Dunham was in Dakar, Senegal, where she was artistic advisor to Senegal's First World Festival of Negro Arts. She has been called the "Marian Anderson of Dance" and continues to discover and encourage black efforts in dance.

Diplomatic Corps

The first Negro to represent the United States abroad officially was Ebenezer D. Bassett. In 1869, he was appointed by President Grant as American Minister Resident to Haiti.

Bassett was born free of a mulatto father and an Indian mother in Litchfield, Connecticut, in 1833. He studied at Wesley Academy, Wilbraham, Massachusetts; Connecticut Normal School; and for a brief period at Yale University. At the time of his appointment as minister resident, he was principal of the Institute for Colored Youth in Philadelphia.

In his position as minister, Bassett set a high standard of achievement. The historian Russell L. Adams has commented: "With honor to himself and satisfaction to his country, he filled the position from 1869 to 1877, which was as long as the combined terms of his white predecessors." In recognition of this work, he was named a member of the American Geographical Society and the Connecticut Historical Society.

See also Ambassadors.

Drama

The first American Negro drama group was the African Company. The company began in 1820, and thus antedated professional Negro minstrels by some forty years. Although only a semiprofessional group, the African Company managed to give performances of Shakespeare and other classics in New York with a fair degree of regularity. Their stage was located in a ramshackle structure called the African Grove at the corner of Bleecker and Mercer streets in lower New York. Here for the first time *Othello* was performed with a Negro in the title role. The performance took place probably in 1821, and the actor was James Hewlett, who later played Richard III in the same theater. Although the audiences were largely black, the *National Advocate* reported that they had "graciously made a partition at the back of the house for the accommodation of whites." It was this company that inspired a Negro youth named Ira Aldridge to become an actor and the first international Negro star.

The first time anywhere in the United States that Negro actors in the dramatic theater commanded the serious attention of the critics and of the general press and public was April 17, 1917, at the Garden Theater in New York City. James Weldon Johnson describes this day as "the date of the most important single event in the entire history of the Negro in the American dramatic theatre." The occasion was the presentation of three plays by the poet Ridgely Torrence, *The Rider of Dreams, Granny Maume,* and *Simon the Cyrenian,* with a cast of Negro actors. George Jean Nathan, leading critic of the day, gave the evening high praise and cited two of the actors, Opal Cooper and Inez Clough, among the top ten performers of the year.

◆

The first play on Broadway which was written by a Negro, was *Appearances,* by Garland Anderson. This play was produced in 1929. Anderson had worked as a bellhop in San Francisco, and made a cross-country auto tour, to publicize his play. Upon his arrival in New York, he was greeted by the mayor in front of City Hall.

See also Actors.

Economics

The first Negro to receive a Ph.D. in economics was Sadie T. M. Alexander. The degree was conferred in 1921 by the University of Pennsylvania. Her dissertation was entitled, "The Standard of Living Among 100 Negro Migrant Families in Philadelphia." Her study was based on personal inquiry into the budgets and living conditions of a hundred families who had moved to the North in 1916, 1917, and 1918, and its purpose was to determine the extent to which these families had been able to adapt to life in an industrial community.

Education

The first school for Negroes and Indians was established in 1620. According to Du Bois, the first schools to be established were private institutions. In New York City, in 1704, a school was

opened for Negroes and Indians by Elias Neau, and in 1750
Anthony Benezet established an evening school for blacks in
Philadelphia.

◆

The first famous Negro educator in the United States was John
Chavis, who was born in Granville County, North Carolina, near
Oxford, in 1753. He was born free and was sent to Princeton,
where he studied privately under Doctor Witherspoon and did
extremely well. Chavis went to Virginia to preach to Negroes. In
1802, in a Virginia court, his freedom and character were certified
to, and it was declared that he had passed "through a regular
course of academic studies" at what is now Washington and Lee
University. In 1805, he was returned to North Carolina, where in
1809 he was ordained a Presbyterian minister and ministered to
whites and slaves in various churches in at least three counties of
North Carolina. Chavis started a college preparatory school for
young white men in North Carolina and had among his students
many who distinguished themselves in the history of North Carolina. These included a United States Senator, a governor of the state,
the sons of a chief justice of North Carolina, and many others.
Some of his pupils boarded with his family, and his school was
regarded as the best in the state. "All accounts agree that John
Chavis was a gentleman." In 1832, as a result of the Nat Turner
insurrection, he was prohibited by law from teaching whites or
preaching to them. Afterward he taught school for free Negroes in
Raleigh. His name is memorialized in the John Chavis Memorial
Park in Raleigh.

◆

The first Negro to receive an honorary degree in the United
States was Lemuel Haynes. He received an honorary A.M. degree
from Middlebury College in 1804. The following information is
taken from the general catalogue of Middlebury College:

> Lemuel Haynes. Born in West Hartford, Conn., July
> 18, 1753. Enlisted as a Minute Man in the Colonial Army,
> 1755; Volunteer in expedition to Ticonderoga, 1776. Sup-
> plied, Congregational Church, Granville, N.Y., 1780. Or-
> dained, 1785. Pastor, Torrington, Conn., 1785–1787; Rut-
> land, Vt., 1787–1818. Removed to Manchester, Vt., 1818.
> Pastor, Granville, N.Y., 1822–1833. Author: "Divine De-

crees, and Encouragement to the Use of Means" and "Universal Salvation." Married Elizabeth Babbat, September, 1783. Died in Granville, N.Y., September 28, 1833, A.M.

◆

The first Negro college graduates were Edward Jones and John Russwurm. Jones graduated from Amherst College on August 23, 1826. Jones had enrolled at Amherst in the second year of its existence—1822. He came from Charleston, South Carolina, where his father, a freedman, was a hotelkeeper and caterer. By the time of his graduation, however, he listed his home as New York. "Though his skin was darker than your own," President Herman Humphrey reminded Amherst alumni, ". . . you treated him as a brother student." After study at Andover Theological Seminary and the African Misson School in Hartford, he was ordained a priest of the Episcopal church in 1830, and at the same time was given an honorary M.A. by Trinity College. According to some sources, he worked first as a missionary in Liberia, but his major effort was to be in the neighboring British colony of Sierra Leone. There, in January, 1841, he became principal of Fourah Bay Christian Institution. In 1848, Fourah Bay Christian Institution took the name "college." The principal and two tutors taught a respectable curriculum, emphasizing mathematics, languages, and theology; but Jones—like the old-time college presidents—seemed to value character-building and soul-saving over intellectual accomplishment. Jones died in England in 1864.

John Russwurm graduated from Bowdoin College in Brunswick, Maine, on September 6, 1826. Three years later, he received his M.A. from Bowdoin. Russwurm became a newspaper editor in New York, and later served as Superintendent of Schools in Liberia. Following that, he served as Colonial Secretary and Governor of the province of Maryland in Liberia.

◆

The first school for Negro girls was St. Francis Academy, established in Baltimore in 1829 by the Colored Woman's Society.

◆

The first school integration lawsuit was filed by Benjamin Roberts on behalf of his daughter in 1840 against the City of

Boston. The Massachusetts Supreme Court rejected the suit, and established the "separate but equal" precedent.

◆

The first known Negro professor to teach in a white college was Charles L. Reason who was called in 1849 to the professorship of mathematics and belles-lettres at New York Central College in McGrawville, New York. The college had been established by abolitionists.

◆

The first Negro institution of higher learning in the United States was Ashnum Institute (afterward Lincoln University). It was founded by Presbyterians in 1854 in Lincoln, Pennsylvania.

◆

The first day school where the freedmen were to receive the rudiments of learning was established on September 17, 1861, in the town of Hampton, Virginia. Its first teacher was Mrs. Mary Peake, a Negro, who taught under the auspices of the American Missionary Association. Around this small school sprung up the other schools in the Hampton vicinity, all of which led to the Hampton Institute of today.

◆

The first Negro woman in the U.S. to receive the A.B. degree was Mary Jane Patterson, who graduated from Oberlin College in 1862. Miss Patterson was born in Raleigh, North Carolina, and was brought to Oberlin in her early youth by her parents, who were probably fugitive slaves. She studied one year in the preparatory department and four years in the college before graduation. Upon receiving her degree, she went to Philadelphia, where she taught in the Institute for Colored Youths for seven years. In 1869 she went to Washington to teach, and in 1871 became the first Negro principal of the newly-established Preparatory High School for Negroes. She held the position until 1884, except for one year, and did much to build up the institution. After her resignation as principal, at which time a Negro man was appointed as her successor, she continued as a teacher in the school until her death in 1894.

◆

The first Negro president of a college was Bishop Daniel Payne. In 1863, he became the president of the newly-incorporated Wilberforce University of the AME Church. Long before he rose to prominence, Payne dreamed of a college where the "Peace of God and the light of learning would shine." A native of Charleston, South Carolina, Daniel Payne attained in his early years the rudiments of an education. Later he continued his studies at a Lutheran Seminary in Gettysburg, Pennsylvania. While president of Wilberforce, he saw many of his charges develop into the capable ministers he thought the church should have.

◆

The first Negro university to establish undergraduate, graduate, and professional schools was Howard University in Washington, D.C., which was founded on November 20, 1866, as the Howard Theological Seminary. On January 8, 1867, the name was changed to Howard University. On May 1, 1867, the Normal Department and the Preparatory Department opened in a leased frame structure with five students, the children of trustees. The school was incorporated on March 2, 1867, by an act of Congress, which authorized the establishment of the Normal and Preparatory, Collegiate, Theological, Medical, Law, and Agricultural departments.

◆

The first Negro to earn a Ph.D. in the United States was Edward Bouchet. This he received in physics from Yale University in 1867, just ten years after the first Ph.D. was awarded by an American school. Not only was he the first Negro to hold a Ph.D. in any field, but he was also the first to be elected to membership in Phi Beta Kappa.

Concerning his life since graduation, Bouchet wrote:

In September, 1876, I began teaching physics and chemistry in the institute for Colored Youth, Philadelphia, Pa., and continued to fill that position until June, 1902. From September, 1902, until November, 1903, I was connected with the Summer High School, St. Louis, Mo., as teacher of physics and mathematics. From November, 1903, until May, 1904, I was business manager for the Provident Hospital, a private institution located in St. Louis, Mo. From May,

1904, until March, 1905, I was United States Inspector of
Customs at the Louisiana Purchase Exposition in St. Louis,
stationed at Ceylon Court. This appointment was obtained
through the good offices of the Honorable Charles F. Joy
and other St. Louis friends. In October, 1906, I became
director of Academics at the St. Paul Normal and Industrial
School, located at Lawrenceville, Va., where I remained
until June, 1908, and in September, 1908, I accepted the
position of principal of the Lincoln High School at Gallipo-
lis, Ohio. My favorite recreations are walking and rowing.
The classmates I have met most frequently have been
George L. Dickerman, Henry W. Farnham, George L. Fox,
George M. Gunn, Charles F. Joy, James C. Sellers and
Edmond Zacher.

The first Negro to receive an honorary degree from Howard
University was Dr. Alexander T. Augusta. He was awarded the
honorary degree—Doctor of Medicine—in 1869 for his outstanding accomplishments in the field of medicine.

The first Negro graduate from Harvard University was Richard T. Greener, who graduated with a B.A. degree in 1870. Born in
Philadelphia and reared in Boston, he attended the common schools
at Cambridge and preparatory school at Oberlin and Phillips
Andover before entering Harvard, where he won the Boylston Prize
in oratory in his sophomore year and again as a senior, as well as
the Bowdoin Prize for a dissertation. Greener served during Reconstruction as a professor of philosophy at the University of South
Carolina, completing a law course there at the same time and
securing admission to the bar of that state and of Washington, D.C.
Upon his return to Washington, he became dean of the Howard
University Law School but resigned to become a law clerk in the
office of the first comptroller of the United States Treasury. He
practiced law privately in Washington from 1882 until he was
appointed U.S. Commercial Agent at Vladivostok, Russia.

The first Negro land-grant college was Alcorn Agricultural and
Mechanical College, which was established by the state of Missis-
sippi in 1871, at Rodney, Mississippi. The original name was
Alcorn University. Hiram Revels, the first Negro elected to the U.S.

Senate, resigned his seat to become Alcorn's first president. Another distinguished Negro American who was outstanding in the history of Alcorn was Major John R. Lynch, then speaker of the Mississippi House of Representatives, who signed the bill for the establishment and creation of Alcorn University.

◆

The first Negro State Superintendent of Public Instruction in Louisiana was William G. Brown. He served in this capacity from 1872 to 1876. During his period of office, Brown fought for complete integration and set up a workable educational system. Before he became superintendent, schools for whites had been very poor, and there were none for Negroes. Brown was not only the first Negro to serve as state superintendent of public instruction but also was the first man of either race to sit as chairman of the first state board of education.

◆

The first Negro State Superintendent of Public Instruction in Florida was Jonathan C. Gibbs. He served in this capacity from 1872 to 1874. Gibbs, a Dartmouth graduate, put stability into the tottering Florida public school system. He succeeded in founding in that state a splendid system of schools, which remained even after the fall of the carpetbag governments. A white historian has said Gibbs was "probably the most outstanding character in the early life of the Florida public school system."

◆

The first Negro State Superintendent of Public Instruction in Arkansas was J. C. Corbin. He was elected to this position in 1873, and served for a period of two years. Corbin, a graduate of the University of Ohio, left office with an impressive record.

◆

The first vocational institute of learning conducted solely by black men for black men was Tuskegee Institute. Opened on July 4, 1881, with a $2,000 appropriation from the Alabama State Legislature, the school consisted of a single shanty, a student body of thirty, and one teacher—Booker T. Washington. Tuskegee functioned originally as a normal school for the training of Negro teachers—the first of its kind established in the United States.

Eventually it came to specialize in agricultural and manual training, areas which were to make both the school and its teacher famous.

◆

The first Negro to receive the Ph.D. from Boston University was Doctor J. E. W. Bowen. He graduated from the School of Theology in 1885.

◆

The first Negro to receive a Ph.D. from Harvard University was W. E. B. Du Bois in 1895. Born in Great Barrington, Massachusetts, on February 23, 1868, Du Bois received a bachelor's degree from Fisk University, and went on to win a second bachelor's degree, as well as a Ph.D., from Harvard. Subsequently he had the satisfaction of seeing his dissertation published as the first volume of a notable series, the *Harvard Historical Studies*. He was for a time professor of Latin and Greek at Wilberforce and a professor of sociology at the University of Pennsylvania; Du Bois also served as a professor of sociology, history, and economics at Atlanta University. He was one of the founders of the NAACP and was the author of twelve books and numerous articles in leading professional journals. His *Souls of Black Folk* was the first great classic on the race question.

◆

The first school in the United States to make a scientific study of the Negro was Atlanta University. According to W. E. B. Du Bois, Atlanta began the scientific study of the American Negro in 1896, before any other institution of learning in America offered a course of lectures on the Negro or made any attempt to measure or study the black man.

◆

The first Negro to receive an honorary degree from Harvard University was Booker T. Washington. On June 24, 1896, he was awarded the honorary degree of Master of Arts. The *Boston Post* wrote:

> In conferring the honorary degree of Master of Arts upon the Principal of Tuskegee Institute, Harvard University has honored itself as well as the object of this distinction.

The work which Prof. Booker T. Washington has accomplished for the education, good citizenship and popular enlightenment in his chosen field of labor in the South entitles him to rank with our national benefactors. The University which can claim him on its list of sons, whether in regular course or *honoris causa* may be proud.

It has been mentioned that Mr. Washington is the first of his race to receive an honorary degree from a New England University. This, in itself, is a distinction. But the degree was not conferred because Mr. Washington is a colored man, or because he was born in slavery, but because he has shown, by his work for the elevation of the people of the Black Belt of the South, a genius and a broad humanity which count for greatness in any man, whether his skin be white or black.

The first Negro president of Morehouse College (founded in 1867) was John Hope, a graduate of Brown University in 1894. In 1906, he was elevated to the presidency after having served as a professor of Latin and Greek at this institution. Later, Hope became president of Atlanta University. Morehouse is today one of the foremost institutions in the South for Negroes.

The first American Negro to receive a Ph.D. degree from a foreign country was Gilbert H. Jones. Jones was born in Fort Mott, South Carolina, on August 23, 1883, and received his degree from Jena University in Germany in 1909. He was president of Wilberforce University from 1924 to 1932, and later returned as dean in the late 1950's. He retired about 1960, and died in June, 1966.

The first Negro to receive a Ph.D. from Columbia University was George Edmund Haynes, a pioneer in American race relations. Born in Pine Bluff, Arkansas, Haynes received a B.A. from Fisk University in 1903, and an M.A. from Yale in 1904. In 1912, he received his Ph.D. from Columbia, where his thesis, *The Negro at Work in New York City,* was published by the university press. In 1910, Haynes was one of the founders of the National Urban League, serving as its executive director for six years. In that same year, he organized the department of social science at Fisk University and was its chairman until 1921. He wrote three important books—*Negro Newcomers in Detroit, The Trend in Race Relations,* and *Africa—Continent of the Future.* He helped organize the department of race relations in the Federal Council of Churches of Christ in America and was appointed the first executive secretary of this organization, a position he held for twenty-six years.

◆

The first Negro woman to earn a Ph.D. degree in the United States was Sadie Alexander, born in Philadelphia, Pennsylvania in 1898. She received her degree in economics in 1921 from the University of Pennsylvania. She was also the first woman to earn a law degree from the University of Pennsylvania. In 1927, she became the first Negro woman to be admitted to the bar in the state of Pennsylvania. Before graduating with honors from the University of Pennsylvania in 1918, Mrs. Alexander had acted as the associate editor of the university's law review. The author of several articles, she was the editor of *Who's Who Among Negro Lawyers* in 1949.

◆

The first and only Catholic institution for the higher education of Negroes in America was Xavier University. It was founded in 1925, in New Orleans, Louisiana, by a Philadelphia heiress, Katherine Drexel, whose father was head of the banking house of Drexel and Morgan. Miss Drexel, later known as Mother M. Katherine, gave up her social heritage and personal fortune to don the simple black robes of a nun and establish, in 1891, the Congregation of the Sisters of the Blessed Sacrament—the first and still the only Catholic order dedicated exclusively to educational and missionary work for the American Negroes and Indians.

◆

The first Negro to receive an honorary degree from Oberlin College was R. Nathaniel Dett. The citation, which Dett received in 1926, reads as follows:

R. NATHANIEL DETT:

> Masterful musical leader and inspiring composer,
> active in the work of Hampton Institute.

*   *   *   *

Mr. Chairman:
> The most beloved of Roman Poets, looking forward to
> an old age he was never destined to attain, prayed for two
> blessings. "May it be granted me, Oh son of Leto, to spend

an old age without disgrace and not without song."

To each race is given its own peculiar gift, each makes its contribution to our complex life and it is the abiding glory of the Negro race that they have given us song. For song as the same poet has said is a "monument more enduring than bronze, unharmed by any wind, or the measureless lapse of years or the flight of time."

It is thus an especial honor to his Alma Mater that a son of Oberlin has attained high distinction in this the most enduring and most subtle of the arts. I have the honor to present for the degree of Doctor of Music, Nathaniel Dett of the Conservatory class of 1908, a choral director and a beloved teacher at Hampton Institute and a composer of songs.

COMMENCEMENT, JUNE 1926

◆

The first Negro president of Howard University was Mordecai Johnson, an eminent Baptist minister. Before assuming the presidency in 1926, he had been a successful Baptist minister in Charleston, West Virginia. Prior to this he had taught economics and history at Morehouse College. Dr. Johnson earned his A.B. degree from Morehouse in 1911; the Master of Sacred Theology degree from Harvard in 1923; and the Doctor of Divinity degree from Gammon Theological Seminary in 1928. Under his administration, Howard University, founded in an abandoned dancehall and beer saloon in 1867, was transformed from a cluster of second-rate departments to an institution of national distinction. The university's school of law is preeminent in the area of civil rights. Its medical school has been turning out half of the Negro physicians in the country. Its Negro Collection, under the supervision of Mrs. Dorothy B. Porter, is one of the finest in the world.

◆

The first Negro president of Atlanta University was John Hope. Hope had previously served as president of Morehouse College. He assumed the position at Atlanta University in 1928.

◆

The first Negro president of Lincoln University (founded in 1854) was Horace Mann Bond. He was elected president of this oldest Negro institution of higher learning for Negroes in 1945. Bond received his A.B. from Lincoln University and his M.A. and

Ph.D. from the University of Chicago. Before coming to Lincoln, he had served as head of the department of education at Langston University, Langston, Oklahoma; Director of Extension at Alabama State College, Montgomery, Alabama; instructor and research assistant at Fisk University; dean of Dillard University, New Orleans, Louisiana; head of the department of English at Fisk University, Nashville, Tennessee; and President of Fort Valley College at Fort Valley, Georgia.

The first Negro named president of Fisk University in Nashville, Tennessee, since it was founded in 1865, was Charles Johnson. Before becoming president of Fisk, in 1946, Dr. Johnson had been head of Fisk's Department of Social Sciences for eighteen years. In this capacity he helped Fisk to remain a leader in the scientific study of race relations in America. Largely through his efforts, the nationally-known Fisk Institute of Race Relations was created.

Johnson was born in Bristol, Virginia, the oldest of five children of the Reverend Charles Henry Johnson, an emancipated slave. As a youth shining shoes in Bristol, he developed the objectivity, the curiosity, and the concern for people which characterized all of his scientific work.

He graduated with a B.A. degree from Virginia Union University in 1916. In 1917, he received a Ph.D. from the University of Chicago. He was awarded honorary doctorates by Harvard, Howard, Columbia, Virginia Union, and the University of Glasgow in Scotland. His death, in 1956, created a void in the study of ethnic relations in America.

The University of Arkansas became the first institution in the Deep South to admit Negro students to regular classes in its graduate schools when, on August 24, 1948, it announced that its freshman medical class entering in September would include Edith Mae Irby of Hot Springs. It was announced at the same time that Miss Irby, twenty years old and a graduate of Knoxville College in Tennessee, ranked twenty-eighth in an aptitude test given to determine the ninety students who would make up the freshman class.

The first Negro to receive an honorary degree from a white college in the South was Mary McLeod Bethune, the founder and president of the coeducational Bethune-Cookman College in Daytona Beach, Florida. On March 1, 1949, she was awarded an honorary degree—Doctor of Humanities—by Rollins College in Winter Park, Florida. Dr. Bethune has been called "The First Lady of Education."

◆

The first Negro to receive an honorary degree from New York University was Channing H. Tobias. His degree was awarded in 1950. During World War II, Tobias was a member of numerous civil rights and governmental advisory committees and, in 1946, was named director of the Phelps-Stokes Fund, a foundation devoted to the improvement of educational opportunities for Negroes. He was a Spingarn medalist and the recipient of numerous other citations.

◆

The first Negro to serve as a school board member in a major deep South city since Reconstruction was Reful E. Clement. In 1953 he was elected to the Atlanta Board of Education and remained a member until his death in 1967. Dr. Clement was dean of Louisville Municipal College from 1931, when it was founded, until 1937, when he accepted the presidency of Atlanta University. He remained at Atlanta University until his death.

◆

The first decision of the Supreme Court declaring segregation in the public schools unconstitutional was *Brown* v. *Board of Education*. On May 17, 1954, Chief Justice Earl Warren delivered the opinion of the Court declaring that segregation in the public schools was unconstitutional. The opinion was unanimous; not even a separate concurrence was written.

"We conclude," Warren said, "that in the field of public education the doctrine of 'separate but equal' [the dictum of the *Plessy* v. *Ferguson* decision of 1896] has no place. Separate educational facilities are inherently unequal."

The *Brown* decision was immediately recognized as a major turning point in the course of Negro history in the United States. The decision itself applied only to schools below the college level but it had unmistable implications for public institutions of higher learning. And it had similar implications for any publicly operated facility—library, museum, beach, park, zoo, golf course, etc. Indeed, the decision could be extended to any field in which segregation was imposed by state law.

The first Negro to head a predominantly and traditionally white college anywhere in the country since 1882 is Dr. James Allen Colston. On September 1, 1966, he was named president of the Bronx (N.Y.) Community College. This institution, which has 2,700 day and 4,500 evening students, is one of six two-year institutions operated as part of the City University, in cooperation with the State University. For fourteen years prior to this appointment he was president of Knoxville (Tennessee) College. Holding degrees from Morehouse College (A.B.), Atlanta University (M.A.), and New York University (Ph.D.), Dr. Colston has done postdoctoral study at the University of Chicago and Columbia University. He is president of the United Presbyterian Men of the U.S.A.

The first Negro president of the National Education Association is Elizabeth Duncan Koontz. She served as a teacher of the mentally retarded in Salisbury, North Carolina, for ten years. She headed North Carolina's all-Negro N.E.A. affiliate and N.E.A.'s division, the Association of Classroom Teachers (820,000 members), before her election in 1967 as N.E.A. president. She is the first Negro to hold both these positions. Mrs. Koontz has also received citations for distinguished professional service and achievements in the field of teaching. At the annual meeting in 1968 of the Association for the Study of Negro Life and History, in New York City, she was given an honorary life membership certificate.

The first Negro to receive an honorary degree from Tulane University was Albert Dent, president of Dillard University. During the June commencement of 1969, he was awarded the honorary degree of Doctor of Laws.

The first Negro assistant dean at Yale University is James A. Thomas, a former staff member of a Senate subcommittee. Thomas was appointed assistant dean of Yale Law School in June, 1969. He is the first Negro member of the university's administration. Thomas is a 1964 graduate of Yale Law School, who immediately went into the U.S. Justice Department's Civil Rights Division. In January, 1969, he became a member of the staff of the Administrative Practice and Procedures Subcommittee of the Senate Judiciary Committee.

◆

The first Negro State Superintendent of Public Instruction since Reconstruction was Dr. John W. Porter, who was appointed by Michigan's Governor William G. Milliken on October 10, 1969.

A native of Fort Wayne, Indiana, Porter holds a B.A. degree from Albion College and both the M.A. and Ph.D. degrees from Michigan State University, where he studied counseling and guidance, research, political science, and personnel work in higher education.

Before joining the department of education of the state of Michigan in 1958, Porter taught social studies at West Junior High School in Lansing, served as counselor, and was an administrative assistant to the principal there. During high school and college, he had worked summers in a steel mill, as a furniture salesman, and as custodian in three elementary schools. He earned all-city honors during high school in football, basketball, and track and, in 1952, was named most valuable player in basketball by the Michigan Intercollegiate Athletic Association. He holds a distinguished service award from the Lansing Branch of the Nation Association for the Advancement of Colored People.

Governor Milliken commented at a press conference that he was "very pleased" with Porter's appointment. "The fact that a man of Dr. Porter's caliber has accepted the position is very encouraging," the Governor said.

◆

The first Negro to become president of a major public university is Dr. Clifton R. Wharton, who was named president of Michigan State University in East Lansing, Michigan. He assumed his duties on January 2, 1970.

Dr. Wharton is a native of Boston and was an honors graduate from Harvard University in 1947. He received master's degrees in economics from Johns Hopkins in 1948, and from the University of Chicago in 1958. He obtained his doctorate in economics from the University of Chicago in 1958. Dr. Wharton has a long list of firsts. He was the first Negro to join the student radio station at Harvard; the first national secretary and one of the founding members of the National Student Association; the first black student at the Johns Hopkins University School of Advanced International Studies; and the first black person to receive a Ph.D. in economics from the University of Chicago. Recently he became the first Negro to be elected a director of the Equitable Life Assurance Society.

◆

The first Negro to be elected president of the National Association for Supervision and Curriculum Development (NASCD) is Dr. Alvin D. Loving, Sr. He is the first black person to achieve the position of a full professor at the University of Michigan in Ann Arbor. Currently professor of education at the University, Dr. Loving was installed at the NASCD national convention in San Francisco in May, 1970.

◆

The first John Dewey Distinguished Service Professor named at the University of Chicago was Dr. Allison Davis, a Negro, who received this honor in 1970. Davis was the first educator to point out the inadequacies of intelligence quotient (I.Q.) tests for accurately measuring the education potential of lower-class children. Dr. Davis, professor of education at the university, wrote the book, *Social Class Influences Upon Learning,* considered a major work in the field, which disproves the previously accepted theories on I.Q. tests. He is also credited with carrying out the first social and anthropological study of modern society based on research in the Southern states. Dr. Davis, who has served on the university's staff since 1942, is also the coauthor of eight books, the latest being *Compensatory Education for Cultural Deprivation* (1965), written with Benjamin Bloom and Robert Hess.

◆

The first Negro to become assistant dean of the Vanderbilt University Divinity School is the Reverend Kelly Miller Smith, who was active in Nashville sit-ins and civil rights protests in the early 1960's. Named to the position in 1970, Smith is the first black person ever to fill an administrative post at Vanderbilt.

The first Negro State Superintendent of Public Instruction in California was Wilson C. Riles. In November, 1970, Riles, an orphan who was reared in the backwoods of Louisiana, polled 3,195,555 votes to the white superintendent Max Rafferty's 2,716,369 in the nonpartisan race. The victory made Riles the first black person elected to a statewide office in California.

In 1940, Riles received his B.A. degree from Northern Arizona University of Flagstaff, Arizona; in 1947, he was awarded the M.A. degree from the same university. Pepperdine University of Los Angeles, California, conferred on him the honorary degree, LL.D., in 1967.

The first public black institutions to enroll more than ten thousand students (1970–71) was Southern University. It has campuses in Baton Rouge, New Orleans, and Shreveport, and is the largest of the predominantly black institutions.

Southern University was organized under constitutional requirement by the Louisiana State Constitutional Convention of 1879, through an article introduced in that body by P. B. S. Pinchback, former black Lieutenant-Governor and Acting Governor of Louisiana.

At present there are thirty-three public black institutions.

See also Rhodes Scholars.

Elective Office

The first Negro to win an elective office in the history of the United States was John Mercer Langston. He was elected clerk of Brownhelm Township, Lorain County, Ohio, in 1855. Upon his graduation from Oberlin in 1853, he was denied entrance to law schools in New York and Ohio, and had to be content to read law in an attorney's office. When he offered himself for the bar, the referees agonized over Langston's eligibility and finally ruled in his favor on the theory that he was more white than black.

The first Negro to be elected to the Aldermanic Board of New York City was Charles H. Roberts, a Republican. Roberts was elected in 1919.

The first Negro to be elected Borough President of Manhattan was Hulan Jack, who was elected to the post in 1953. Jack, a Democrat, had previously served as a state assemblyman for thirteen years and was backed in his contest by the Tammany Hall organization.

The first Negroes elected to office in Alabama in this century were the Reverend K. L. Buford and Stanley Smith, who became members of the Tuskegee City Council in 1964.

See also Congress; Governors; Mayors; State Legislatures.

Emancipation Proclamation

See Abolitionism.

Engineering

The first known Negro to receive a Ph.D. in engineering from California Institute of Technology was Ronald McLaughlin, a Canadian citizen. He received his M.S. in Civil Engineering in 1952, and his Ph.D. in 1958.

The first black engineer to be accorded distinction and honor for excellence in his field was D. N. Crosthwait, P.E. (Professional Engineer), of Michigan City, Indiana. He was among over twenty engineers so honored at the meeting of the American Society of Heating, Refrigeration and Air Conditioning Engineers at the Bellevue-Stratford Hotel in Philadelphia, on January 26, 1971. Crosthwait also has the distinction of being the only black engineer so honored by the Society in its seventy-six years of existence.

He was raised to the Fellow grade of membership, which recognizes attaintment of "unusual distinction in the relating to the sciences of heating, refrigeration and air-conditioning or ventilation, and for substantial contribution to such arts and sciences."

Crosthwait, who finished grade and high schools in Kansas City, Missouri, holds the B.S. in Mechanical Engineering and the professional degree of Mechanical Engineering from Purdue University.

After graduation he was active with the design, installation, testing and balancing, and servicing of power plants, heating and ventilating systems. Thirty-four U.S. patents and about eighty foreign patents have been granted Crosthwait. He has also made numerous contributions to trade and technical publications.

Crosthwait is registered as a professional mechanical and electrical engineer by Iowa, Indiana, and Illinois societies of Professional Engineers, the American Society of Heating, Refrigeration and Air-Conditioning Engineers, the American Chemical Society, and the Iowa Academy of Sciences.

He is a member and Fellow of the American Association for the Advancement of Science, the past president and a former member of the Michigan City Urban Renewal Commission, and is listed in *Who's Who in Engineering,* the biographical dictionary of American men of sciences.

See also Inventions.

Episcopal Church

The first Negro Episcopal church was organized by Absalom Jones in Philadelphia in 1794. Jones's followers held their first meetings in the homes of such stalwarts as Elder John Emory and Deacon Caesar Worthington; they finally purchased a 40-by-60-foot lot on the southwest corner of Fifth and Adelphi streets, and erected there a "substantial" building containing 160,000 bricks. Said Jones: "We dedicate ourselves to God and our house to the memory of Saint Thomas the Apostle, to be henceforth known and called Saint Thomas African Episcopal Church of Philadelphia." St. Thomas Episcopal Church is currently located in West Philadelphia, at 52nd and Parrish streets, over sixty blocks away from the original site.

The first Negro Episcopal bishop of the American church was Reverend Samuel David Ferguson, who was elected to the House of Bishops of the Protestant Episcopal Church in 1884. He was consecrated on June 24, 1885, at Grace Church in New York City, as the successor of the Missionary Bishop of Liberia.

The first Negro Episcopal bishop to serve in the United States was the Right Reverend Edward T. Demby, who was appointed suffragan bishop among the Negroes in Arkansas and the Southwest on September 29, 1918. He served from 1918 to 1939.

The first Negro Episcopal bishop to serve a predominantly white diocese was the Right Reverend John M. Burgess, who was elected in September, 1962, as suffragan bishop of the Diocese of Massachusetts. Bishop Burgess did advanced study in sociology at the University of Michigan before graduating from the Episcopal Theological Seminary at Cambridge, Massachusetts, in 1934. After his ordination, he served a clerical apprenticeship at churches in Grand Rapids, Michigan, and Cincinnati, Ohio. In 1946, he was called to the chaplaincy of Washington's Howard University, and five years later he became canon of Washington Cathedral. Until his consecration, Burgess was Archdeacon of Boston and supervisor of the Episcopal City Missions. He has chosen for the suffragan bishropic over four white candidates on the first ballot at a convention of diocesan priests.

"The church," Bishop Burgess has commented, "should try to make religion relevant to the needs of all kinds of people. The church is not a sect organized around a particular doctrine or Biblical text. It is a great fellowship bound by loyalty to Christ."

The first cathedral in the Episcopal church to be fully integrated was Trinity Cathedral in Newark, New Jersey. Trinity Cathedral gained wide attention in October, 1966, when it merged with Saint Paul's Episcopal Church, a predominantly Negro congregation.

◆

The first black bishop coadjutor in the history of the Episcopal Church was the Right Reverend John M. Burgess, who had served as suffragan bishop of Massachusetts since 1962. He was elected in June, 1969, in a special convocation of the Episcopal Diocese of Massachusetts held at Northeastern University's Alumni Hall. Bishop Burgess topped eleven candidates for the post and was elected on the fifth ballot.

The diocese of Massachusetts is one of the first Episcopalian dioceses established in the United States; it is now the sixth largest, with a membership of about 125,000 parishioners.

◆

The first Negro dean of a cathedral of the Episcopal Church in the United States is Canon Dillard Robinson, who was elected to the deanship of the Trinity Cathedral in Newark, New Jersey, in 1969.

Explorations

The first Negro to land in the New World was the navigator of the *Nina,* one of Columbus' ships. Alonzo Pietro, the pilot of his flagship on the first voyage, is mentioned nine times as being a Negro—"Alonzo, the Negro," "the Negro, Alonzo"—in the *Libretto,* and written by Peter Martyr after interviews with Columbus and his men and published in 1504.

◆

The first crop of wheat in the New World was planted and harvested by Negro explorers with Cortez. Carrido, who was a soldier under Cortez, the conqueror of Mexico in 1521, had brought the grains of wheat in his knapsack from Spain. He sowed them as an experiment and thus became the pioneer of wheat-raising in the western hemisphere.

◆

The first Negroes to come into the United States were brought in as slaves by Lucas Vasquez de Ayllòn, the Spanish explorer who tried to establish a settlement in the Carolinas in 1526. The

Negroes eventually escaped from the settlement and lived with the Indians in the wilderness.

◆

The first man to behold what is now Arizona and New Mexico, except for the aborigines, was the Negro, Estavanico—scout, guide, and ambassador for the explorers Navaez and Cabeza de Vaca. In March, 1539, with Estavanico as guide, a party of three Spaniards and a group of Pima Indians set out in search of the fabled Seven Cities of Cibola. Estavanico never found these nonexistent places, but his explorations led him into what is now Arizona and New Mexico, of which states he is the discoverer.

◆

The historic Lewis and Clark expedition of 1803, which was the first to explore the Western wilderness all the way to the Pacific, had as a member a Negro with the single name of York. He was the "black servant" of Captain William Clark and he was a "remarkable, stout, strong Negro," according to journals describing the voyage. York served as guide and scout, and as boatman on the journey up the Missouri River. He also took his turn at provisioning the expedition, hunting buffalo, bear, deer, and other game.

◆

The first man to reach the North Pole was a Negro explorer, Matthew Alexander Henson. He is considered along with Rear Admiral Robert E. Peary as the codiscoverer of the North Pole. Henson was born in Charles County, Maryland, in 1866.

Henson was chosen by Peary to be a member of the party of six to make the final dash to the Pole. Peary paid him this compliment: "He is my most valuable companion. I could not get along without him." Overcome with exhaustion and crippled by the loss of most of his toes by frostbite, Peary sent Henson forward to make final observations and calculations and to await Peary's arrival. Fully forty-five minutes ahead of the commodore, Henson reached the North Pole by sled on April 7, 1909, and became the first human in history to set foot there. When the expedition finally succeeded in reaching the North Pole, Matthew Henson was given the honor of planting the first American flag on the site.

In recognition of his contributions, Henson was awarded the master of science degree by Morgan State College and Howard

University, a Congressional Medal, life membership in the Explorers Club, a citation by the U.S. Department of Defense, and a gold medal from the Chicago Geographical Society bearing the inscription: " 'I can't get along without him'—Peary." A building at Dillard University in New Orleans in named for Henson, as well as a public school in Chicago. In 1961, Henson's home state paid him tribute on a plaque placed at the State House in Annapolis, identifying him as codiscoverer of the North Pole. Henson is the author of the book, *A Negro Explorer at the North Pole*. He died on March 9, 1955, in New York City.

Expositions

The first public display of Negro achievement in arts, inventions, and handicrafts was at the World's Cotton Exposition, which was held in New Orleans from November, 1884, to May, 1885. Blanche K. Bruce, former U.S. Senator from Mississippi, a Negro, had charge of the Negro exhibit. Owing to Bruce's efforts, the exhibition received much favorable comment from the press. A white Southerner recalled, after many years, the creditable work of Bruce at that time, saying that "he was indefatigable and took becoming pride in seeing his people get their just dues, and that work they had done for freedom would show up well."

Film

The first exposition devoted to the progress of the Negro since slavery was held in Chicago, Illinois, during August and September, 1914. B. B. Mosely, Julius F. Taylor, and W. M. Farmer were the individuals chiefly responsible for the exposition. Mrs. Ida Wells Barnett was named the head of the women's section.

◆

The first black American film director was Melvin Van Peebles. He is the only black director to have made more than two films, and he is one of only three black Americans who have directed movies. (The others were Ossie Davis, who directed *Cotton Comes to Harlem*, and Gordon Parks, who has made *The Learning Tree* and *Shaft*.)

Van Peebles' first film was a French entry in the San Francisco Film Festival, *Story of a Three-Day Pass.* His other films were *Watermelon Man,* and *Sweet Sweetback's Baadasssss Song.*

See also Actors.

Football

The first football game between Negro colleges was played in January, 1897, at Brisbine Park, Atlanta, Georgia. The game was played between Atlanta University and Tuskegee Normal and Industrial Institute. Atlanta won, 10–0. Atlanta's captain was George F. Porter, and Tuskegee's captain was Clarence Matthews.

◆

The first Negro to play football in a primarily white college was Bobby Marshall, of the University of Minnesota, who played in 1905–6. The Minnesota team was known as the Golden Gophers. He was elected to the College Hall of Fame for 1971. A gifted end, Marshall was one of America's first great black athletes. He continued to play football in his fifties with Yale's immortal Pudge Heffelfinger and others in the Minneapolis area. Minnesota athletic director M. W. Ryman marveled as a boy at Marshall's ability and enthusiasm for the game. Marshall's clutch field goal—a goal kicked over the goalpost when the game appeared to be lost—in the mud and rain enabled the Golden Gophers to upset Alonzo Stagg's Chicago powerhouse, which was quarterbacked by Walter Eckersall.

◆

The first known Negro to play professional football was Fritz Pollard of Brown University, who began playing in 1919.

The first Negro to be enshrined in the Football Hall of Fame at Rutgers University was Fred Wayman Slater. Popularly known as "Duke," he was selected as all-American tackle by Walter Eckersall of the *Chicago Tribune* (the former Chicago quarterback) in 1921; as all-time all-American by Pop Warner, in *Colliers* in 1931; and as all-time all-American tackle by a poll of six hundred U.S. sports writers sponsored by the *Chicago Herald-American* in 1946. Slater was selected judge of the municipal court in Chicago in 1948.

◆

The first known Negro quarterback to play in an NFL game was Willie Thrower from Michigan State, who played one game for the Chicago Bears during the 1953 season.

Fraternal Societies

The first Negro Mason in the United States was Prince Hall. He was initiated on March 6, 1775, in an army lodge (No. 441) stationed at Castle William under General Thomas Gage in or near Boston, Massachusetts, although he was at that time a civilian. When the Revolutionary War broke out Prince Hall became a soldier and fought with distinction. Upon the British evacuation of Boston, Prince Hall and his fellow members were given a permit to meet as a lodge. Under the terms of this permit, African Lodge No. 1 was formed on July 3, 1776. On June 30, 1784, after the Revolution, Prince Hall and his fellow Masons applied to the Grand Lodge of England for a warrant, which was issued on September 29, 1784, to African Lodge No. 459, with Prince Hall as Master. The first meeting under the charter was held on May 6, 1787, in Boston.

Hall's interests were not restricted to Lodge activities. He took a deep interest in the general condition of Negroes in Boston and elsewhere. As early as 1776, he urged the Massachusetts legislature to support the cause of emancipation. He successfully prodded the city of Boston to provide schools for free Negro children in 1797. He also served as a preacher in the Methodist Church.

While today's Prince Hall Masons are distinctive because of their peculiar dress and unique public ceremonies, they hold few basic secrets that are not already known to any child of Sunday school age, namely a belief in a supreme being, brotherly love, and relief to the less fortunate. Theirs is a religious order often described as "a system of morality based on allegory and illustrated by symbols."

◆

The first Odd Fellows Lodge, known as the First Colored Lodge, was organized under the leadership of Peter Ogden in 1843. It received its charter directly from England. The lodge became the strongest of the Negro fraternal groups.

◆

The first Elk organization among Negroes had its beginning in Cincinnati, Ohio, during the closing years of the nineteenth century. The idea was conceived by Arthur J. Riggs, a Pullman porter, who formed the Order of Elks among Negroes in February, 1897. At the same time, a similar idea was taking form in the mind of Benjamin Franklin Howard of Covington, Kentucky. The two men met on a Cincinnati street, and Negro Elkdom was born. Officially, the Improved Benevolent and Protective Order of Elks of the World was founded in 1898 by Attorney Howard, who became the first Grand Exalted Ruler of the First Lodge, Cincinnati Lodge 1. Shortly after, the ritual of the IBPOE of W was copyrighted by Mr. Riggs on September 28, 1898. The following year, in June, 1899, the first charter and articles of incorporation were granted. From these humble beginnings, the Negro Elks became known as the largest fraternal organization in the world.

The purpose of the IBPOE of W was "That the welfare and happiness of its members be promoted and enhanced; that nobleness of soul and goodness of heart be cultivated; that the principles of charity, justice, brotherly love, and fidelity be inculcated; that its members and families be assisted and protected; and that the spirit of patriotism be enlivened and exalted."

Fraternities

The first intercollegiate Greek-letter fraternity in the United States for Negro college men was Alpha Phi Alpha Fraternity, founded at Cornell University in Ithaca, New York, on December 4, 1906. The founders of the fraternity were: George B. Kelley, Henry A. Collis, Charles H. Chapman, Nathaniel A. Murray, Bertner W. Tandy, Robert H. Ogle, and James H. Morton, who were students at Cornell. The fraternity grew out of a social study club formed by these students in 1905. The first certificate of incorporation was filed with the Secretary of the State of New York on January 29, 1908. The purpose of the fraternity was declared to be "education and the mutual uplift of its members."

The first general convention was assembled on December 28, 1908, at Howard University in Washington, D.C. The convention expressed hope that "the influence of Alpha Phi Alpha would extend to every Negro college and university in the land, to bring together under one band and with one bond of fraternal love all the worthy leading college men wherever found, to form, as it was, a link to join them together." The constitution, ritual, and plans for expansion were drawn up at this time.

The first issue of the fraternity magazine, *The Sphinx*, was published in February, 1914, containing news of interest to the fraternity, personal notes, and editorials.

◆

The first scholastic fraternity chapter established at a Negro university was formed on April 4, 1953, by Phi Beta Kappa at Fisk University in Nashville, Tennessee. Goodrich Cook, white, president of the United Chapters of Phi Beta Kappa, presented the charter to eight charter members and two foundation members, both Fisk alumni. Four days later a chapter was established at Howard University in Washington, D.C.

Freedmen's Bureau

The first Freedmen's Bureau was created by an act of Congress on March 3, 1865, which was signed by President Abraham Lincoln. Its purpose was to establish schools and improve the economic conditions of the freedmen. It also provided hospitals and acted as a legal guardian to the newly-emancipated blacks. Unlike most of the other aid societies, the Freedmen's Bureau extended considerable assistance to the impoverished white.

Geography

The first black president of the Gamma Theta Upsilon International Honorary Geographical Society was Dr. Theodore R. Speigner, chairman of the Department of Geography of North Carolina Central University in Durham, North Carolina.

Dr. Speigner is the sponsor of the Gamma Pi chapter of Gamma Theta Upsilon located at North Carolina Central University. He earned his A.B. degree at Talladega College; his A.M. at the University of Iowa; and his Ph.D. at the University of Michigan.

The purposes of the Society are:

1. To further professional interest in geography by affording a common organization for those interested in this field.
2. To strengthen student and professional training through academic experiences other than those of the classroom and laboratory.
3. To advance the status of geography as a cultural and practical discipline for study and investigation.
4. To create and administer a loan fund for furthering graduate study and/or research in the field of geography.

Gold Mining

The first Negro gold miner in California was Walter Jackson, who began mining at Downieville, California in 1849. The lure of gold brought several hundred Negroes to the West Coast during the rush of '49.

Golf

The first Negro to play the Professional Golfers' Association tour was Ted Rhodes. He served for nine years, from 1945 to 1954, as personal golf professional to the former heavyweight boxing champion, Joe Louis. Rhodes died in 1969 at the age of fifty-six.

◆

The first Negro to win a major golf tournament was Charles Sifford of Philadelphia. He won the Long Beach Open in 1957.

Governors

The first Negro lieutenant governor elected in the United States and the first black man in America to hold an executive position in a state was Oscar James Dunn. He served as lieutenant governor of Louisiana from 1868 to 1871. Ex-Governor Warmoth, under whom Dunn served, commented that Dunn was a man of commanding personality, fine native ability, and poise. His sudden death on November 21, 1871, in the midst of considerable political turbulence, led to the suspicion that he might have been poisoned. The coroner's decision was that he died from cerebral hemorrhage. Dunn was acting governor for the period of Governor Warmoth's forced absence from the State for several months because of illness.

The first Negro to serve as chief executive of an American state was P. B. S. Pinchback, who was lieutenant governor of Louisiana from December 9, 1872, to January 13, 1873. Governor Henry Warmoth had been impeached, found guilty, and removed from office. Pinchback was sworn in to finish the term as governor. His thirty-six days in office were filled with activity aimed at restoring free elections and civil rights in Louisiana.

◆

The first Negro governor appointed by the President of the United States was William H. Hastie, who was appointed governor of the Virgin Islands by President Harry S Truman. Hastie was inaugurated on May 7, 1946, at Charlotte Amalie, St. Thomas, Virgin Islands.

◆

The first elected black governor of the Virgin Islands was Dr. Melvin H. Evans, a cardiologist-turned-politician, and a long-time Democrat-turned-Republican. He was elected during the gubernatorial election in November, 1970. Originally President Nixon had appointed Evans as the Virgin Island's first native-born black governor. His recent election confirmed islanders' approval of measures taken during his previous months in office.

Evans was born in St. Croix, Virgin Islands. He received his M.D. degree from the Howard University Medical School in 1944.

◆

The first Negro since Reconstruction appointed to a major staff position in the Governor's office was James E. Clyburn who on December 22, 1970, was appointed assistant to the Governor for human resources by Governor John C. West of South Carolina. Clyburn, a resident of Charleston, executive director of the South Carolina Commission of Farm Workers, Inc., and one of the founders of the black-oriented United Citizens party, will coordinate programs in the area of human resources development and handle liaison with agencies administering human resource programs.

◆

The first black governor since Reconstruction and the first black governor of Illinois was Senator Cecil Partee, president pro tem. of the Illinois senate. Partee ascended the governor's chair briefly one morning in early 1971, while both Governor Richard B. Ogilvie and Lieutenant Governor Paul Simon were out of the state. As acting governor (from 9:15 A.M. to 11:00 A.M.), he was paid proportionately for that period, and a letter was sent to the secretary of state and to the auditor of public accounts notifying them to contact Partee for official matters during that time.

Hall of Fame

The first Negro to be elected to the Hall of Fame for great Americans at New York University was Booker T. Washington, educator, who was born in Franklin County near Hale's Ford, Virginia, about April 5, 1858, and died at Tuskegee Institute in Alabama, on November 14, 1915. He was elected in 1945 by fifty-seven votes. The unveiling of his bust took place on May 23, 1946, in the auditorium of the library of New York University at University Heights in New York City.

After graduating with honors at Hampton in 1875, Washington taught school at Maiden, West Virginia, and later studied at Wayland Seminary in Washington, D.C. In 1879, he was appointed instructor at Hampton, where he had the responsibility of training seventy-five Indians. In 1881, with the aid of General Samuel Chapman, the principal of Hampton Institute, Washington set out to organize Tuskegee Institute. He became its first principal and teacher. Recognizing the importance of industrial and agricultural training for the American Negro, he emphasized these skills in the curriculum. His work here earned him national and international recognition. In 1901 he wrote his autobiography, *Up From Slavery*. In addition, he edited *Tuskegee and Its People* (1905), and was the author of several other books, among them *The Future of the American Negro* (1899), *The Life of Frederick Douglass* (1907), *The Story of the Negro* (1909), and *My Larger Education* (1911).

History

The first major history of the black people, *The Origin and History of the Colored People,* was written in 1841 by James W. C. Pennington. An illiterate slave blacksmith in the South, he escaped, learned to read and write in English, Greek, Latin, and German, and won his Doctor of Divinity at the University of Heidelberg in Germany.

◆

The first serious historian of the Negro race, according to John Hope Franklin, was George Washington Williams. In 1868, Williams enrolled in the Newton Theological Seminary and pursued his studies there until he was graduated in 1874, thereby becoming the first Negro alumnus of that institution. Williams developed a profound interest in Negro history. From 1876 to 1883 he diligently carried on his investigations of the Negro's past and finally published his two-volume *History of the Negro Race in America from 1619 to 1880.* The work caused intense excitement in scholarly circles and was generally regarded as the best book on Negro history published during the nineteenth century. Five years later he published his *History of Negro Troops in the War of the Rebellion.* Williams died in 1891, while living in Blackpool, England.

◆

The first Negro to earn a Ph.D. in history was W. E. B. Du Bois. He received this from Harvard University in 1895.

◆

The first scientific historical monograph written by a Negro appeared in 1896. It was W. E. B. Du Bois's *The Suppression of the African Slave Trade, 1638–1870,* which became the first work in the Harvard Historical Studies. It was a landmark in the intellectual growth of the American Negro and is still regarded favorably by serious students of history.

◆

The founder and first executive director of the Association for the Study of Negro Life and History was Carter G. Woodson. The Association was organized at the Wabash Avenue YMCA in Chicago on September 9, 1915. Its purposes are: (1) To promote historical research and writing; (2) To publish books on Negro life and history; (3) To promote the study of the Negro through schools, colleges, churches, homes, fraternal groups, and clubs; (4) The collection of historical manuscripts and materials relating to the Negro people throughout the world; and (5) To bring about harmony between the races and acceptance by interpreting the history of one to the other.

Carter G. Woodson was born in New Canton, Virginia, the son of former slaves. Finishing four years of high school work in a year and a half, he went on to attend Berea College, Lincoln University (Pa.), the University of Chicago, and Harvard University. He received his Bachelor's and Master's degrees from the University of Chicago in 1907 and 1908, and his Doctor's degree from Harvard in 1912. Between 1908 and 1918, Woodson taught high school in Washington, D.C. After serving as dean of the school of liberal arts at Howard and later at West Virginia State College, he quit teaching to devote his time to studying and writing Negro history. Among his books are: *The Education of the Negro Prior to 1861; A Century of Negro Migration; The Negro in Our History; Negro Makers of History; The Story of the Negro Retold; The Mind of the Negro as Reflected in Letters Written During the Crisis of 1800–1861; Negro Orators and Their Orations;* and *The History of the Negro Church.*

In 1916, Woodson brought out the first number of *The Journal of Negro History,* a scholarly repository of research which is used by students throughout the world. This scientific magazine has been published regularly every quarter since 1916.

Woodson brought out the first number of *The Negro History Bulletin* on October 1, 1937. It has been published monthly, October through May, since that date. Woodson also originated the first celebration of Negro History Week on February 7, 1926. Its celebration has continued annually since.

◆

The first Negro department head at the University of Chicago was John Hope Franklin. He became chairman of the sixty-man history department in October, 1967. Franklin, who was born in Rentiesville, Oklahoma, graduated from Fisk in 1935, and took his M.A. and Ph.D. at Harvard. He moved to Washington and taught at Howard, then went to New York as chairman of the history department of Brooklyn College, and fitted in a year as Pitt

Professor of American History at the University of Cambridge in England. He joined the Chicago faculty in 1964.

Dr. Franklin has written *The Emancipation Proclamation, The Militant South, The Negro and the Reconstruction,* and *From Slavery to Freedom.* He recently collaborated with other writers on *Land of the Free,* a high school history text giving recognition to Negro achievements in history.

Commenting on his new position, Dr. Franklin said he had been attracted to the University of Chicago because of its "great tradition in the field of history."

John Hope Franklin also has the honor of being the first Negro president of the Southern Historical Society. He was elected president at its annual meeting in Louisville, Kentucky, in December, 1970.

Horse Racing

The horse that won the first Kentucky Derby, Aristides, was ridden in that race by a Negro jockey, Oliver Lewis, in 1875.

Insurance Companies

The first Negro organization in the United States approximating the nature of an insurance agency was The Free African Society. The founding of this society in Philadelphia, Pennsylvania, in 1778 was probably the first manifestation of independent economic cooperation among Negroes. The purpose of this group was to look after their sick, care for their poor, and bury their dead. The leaders of the organization were persons of prominence. Among the charter members were Richard Allen, the founder of the African Methodist Episcopal church, and Absolom Jones, the most distinguished Negro preacher of the Episcopal church at that time. The fees and benefits of the organization were small. Persons found guilty of drunkenness or disorderly conduct were to be suspended; delinquent members were to be dropped; widows were to be cared for; children of deceased members were given the rudiments of an education.

The Free Society was the precursor of a larger and more impressive institution. "The year 1810," according to Du Bois, "witnessed the creation of the African Insurance Company which was located at number 150 (529) Lombard Street; Joseph Randolph, President; Carey Porter, Treasurer; William Coleman, Secretary; with a capital stock of $5,000." The members of this company were all black people, according to the directories of 1811 and 1813.

Inventions

According to the opinion of Henry E. Baker, an examiner in the United States Patent Office, slaves in the South, experimenting with the separation of the seed from cotton, made the first appliances which, when observed by Eli Whitney, were assembled by him as the cotton gin.

◆

The first Negro to engage in clockmaking in the American colonies was Benjamin Banneker, a noted astronomer, mathematician, and linguist. He was the son of a native African slave and a free mulatto woman and attended an integrated private school through the eight grade. He lived and worked in Baltimore, Maryland, about 1734–1806.

When Banneker was a young man, he acquired a watch from a trader. He had never seen a clock; yet he made one, based on drawings he had done from the watch—a wooden "striking" clock so accurate that it kept perfect time for more than twenty years.

When Banneker died in 1806, he was eulogized before the French Academy by the Marquis de Condorcet, and William Pitt placed his name in the records of the English Parliament.

◆

The first known Negro to be granted a patent in the U.S. was Henry Blair. On October 14, 1834, Blair was granted a patent for corn-planting machine, and, two years later, a second patent for a similar device used in planting cotton. In the registry of the Patent Office, Blair was designated "a colored man"—the only instance of identification by race in these early records. Since that time, over fifteen thousand patents have been granted to Negroes.

◆

The first practical multiple-effect vacuum evaporator for the refining of sugar was invented in 1845 by Norbert Rillieux, Negro engineer, inventor, and scientist of pre-Civil War days. This invention revolutionized the contemporary method of refining sugar and gave the United States sugar industry supremacy in the world. Among American authorities, Charles A. Brown, eminent sugar chemist of the U.S. Department of Agriculture, says: "I have always held that Rilleux's invention is the greatest in the history of American chemical engineering and I know of no other invention that has brought so great a saving to all branches of chemical engineering." A bronze plaque was designed and cast in Amsterdam, and placed in the Louisiana State Museum, which is housed in the old *Cabildo* in New Orleans. The tablet shows a bust of the inventor with the inscription:

To honor and commemorate
Norbert Rillieux
Born at New Orleans, Louisiana
March 18, 1806
Died at Paris, France
October 9, 1894.
Inventor of Multiple Evaporation and its
application into the Sugar Industry.
This tablet was dedicated in 1934 by Corporations representing the Sugar Industry
all over the World

Among Rillieux's other known achievements was the development of a practicable scheme for a system of sewerage for the city of New Orleans, but realization of this project was prevented by the refusal of the authorities to accord to a Negro such an honor as would be conveyed through the acceptance and adoption of his plan.

◆

The first man to direct attention to the need for facilitating the lubrication of machinery was Elijah McCoy, a Negro, who was born in Canada, but lived most of his life in Ypsilanti, Michigan. He completed and patented his first lubricating cup in 1872, and then made some seventy different inventions relating principally to the automatic lubrication of machinery with intermittent drops from a cup so as to avoid the necessity for stopping the machine to oil it. His lubricating cup was in quite general use on the locomotives of the railroads in the Northwest, on steamers of the Great Lakes, and in up-to-date factories throughout the country. "The real McCoy," is often attributed to a slogan coined by his firm.

In 1920, McCoy organized his own company, the Elijah McCoy Manufacturing Company at Detroit, Michigan. He died in 1929, and is buried in Detroit.

◆

The person who executed the drawings for the first telephone and assisted in preparing the applications for the telephone patents of Alexander Graham Bell was Lewis Howard Latimer, a Negro. He became the chief draftsman for the General Electric and Westinghouse Companies.

Born in Chelsea, Massachusetts, on September 4, 1848, Latimer enlisted in the Union navy at the age of fifteen, and on his completion of military service began the study of drafting. In 1881, he invented the first incandescent electric light bulb with a carbon filament. Later, as an engineer for the Edison Company, Latimer assisted in installing and placing in operation some of the first "Maxim" incandescent electric light plants in New York, Philadelphia, London, and certain Canadian cities, and then supervised the production of the carbon filaments employed therein, such as those in the Equitable Building, Fiske & Hatch, Caswell-Massey, and the Union League Club of New York City, as well as the offices of the Philadelphia *Ledger* in that town. Latimer also wrote the first textbook on the lighting system used by the Edison Company.

Latimer died at his home in Flushing, New York, on December 11, 1928.

◆

The inventor of a machine for lasting shoes was Jann E. Matzeliger, a Negro. This was the first invention of its kind capable of performing all steps required to hold a shoe on its last, grip and pull the leather down around the heel, guide and drive the nails into place, and then discharge the shoe as a completed product from the machine. In 1883, Matzeliger applied for a patent, but the device was so complicated that patent reviewers in Washington were unable to understand the diagrams. They dispatched a man to inspect the actual model before granting a patent on it.

This patent was bought by Sidney Winslow and on it was built the great United Shoe Machinery Company—a multimillion-dollar industry. Since the formation of this company in 1890, American shoe production has increased enormously. The cost of shoes was cut in half, the quality greatly improved, the wages of workers increased, the hours of labor diminished, and all these factors have made the Americans the best shod people in the world.

Matzeliger was born in Dutch Guiana, the son of a Negro woman and her husband, a Dutch engineer. He came to America as a young man and worked as a cobbler in Philadelphia and Lynn, Massachusetts. He died of tuberculosis in 1889, at the age of thirty-seven, before he realized the value of his invention. Later a statue was erected in Lynn to honor Matzeliger's memory.

The first great Negro electrical inventor was Granville T. Woods. He patented more than fifty devices relating to electricity, as well as such inventions as a steam boiler furnace, the subject of his first patent, which was obtained in 1884. Woods later broadened his field of inventions and secured patents for transmitting messages between moving trains, and for a number of other transmitters. He patented fifteen inventions for electric railways and as many more various devices for electrical control and distributions. Other inventions included an incubator and automatic airbrakes.

In the earlier stages of his career, Woods organized the Woods Electric Company of Cincinnati, Ohio. This company took over by assignment many of his early patents, but as inventions began to multiply and his fame increased, some of the largest and most prosperous technical and scientific corporations in the United States sought his patents. A perusal of the records in the U.S. Patent Office indicates that many of Woods' inventions were assigned to the General Electric Company of New York, Westinghouse Airbrake Company of Pennsylvania, the American Bell Telephone Company of Boston, and the American Engineering Company.

Woods died on January 30, 1910, in the city of New York, where he had carried on his business for several years preceding his death.

Jewish Negroes

The first Jewish Negro in North America was probably a man named Solomon, who was described as a "mulata Jue." He was arrested in the town of Wenham, Massachusetts, on his way to New Hampshire and Maine for the crime of profaning the Lord's Day by traveling on a Sunday.

◆

The first recorded black Jewish congregation in the United States with a black spiritual leader was the Morrish Zionist Temple. This temple was founded in New York City, in 1899, and its leader was Rabbi Leon Reichelieu. Rabbi Reichelieu said he had been converted to Judaism and had studied under the Orthodox Jewish Yeshivot system. He further said he had been ordained under the ancient tradition of "the laying on of the hands." This custom is also practiced among Ethiopian Jews. Rabbi Reichelieu died in 1964, and was buried in a Jewish cemetery.

◆

The first chief Rabbi of the Ethiopian Hebrew Congregation in the Western Hemisphere is Rabbi Wentworth Arthur Matthew, who was born on June 23, 1892. Some authorities list him as having been born in Lagos, West Africa; others give his birth place as the British West Indies. Rabbi Matthew has devoted over fifty years to bringing the spiritual message of Judaism to black Jewish communities in many urban centers. He is considered the best orator and most capable among the black Jewish Rabbis. According to one study appearing in the publication *Judaism* Matthew came to New York in 1913, at a time when, because of a large-scale immigration of Negroes from the South and the West Indies to the northern urban centers, the Negroes naturally felt insecure in their new surroundings. The time was right for spiritual leaders to arise. There was also a very large number of black females in the new environment. The frequent occurrence of a large percentage of women in churches and synagogues was a positive ingredient to any beginning congregation.

On June 25, 1966, the Commandment Keepers' Ethiopian Hebrew Congregation, of which Matthew is spiritual leader, celebrated a golden anniversary by holding a banquet in honor of its Rabbi. The journal describing this gala evening makes the following observations regarding Rabbi Matthew:

> Rabbi Mathew inaugurated the Ethiopian Hebrew Rabbinical College. He has ordained a goodly number of well-trained Rabbis, elders and graduate students of the Hebrew School. His leadership has produced many educated members of all areas, a Home for the Aged, a growing Hebrew Community Center in New York City and Babylon, Long Island. He is now trying to establish a village in Israel

in the name of the Falasha Hebrews in the Western Hemisphere, under his leadership. We are proud to say his sacrifices have met with great success, his marriage is also a success and his ministry has proven a success.

◆

The first Committee on the Black Jews of the Federation of Jewish Philanthropies was formed in 1964, with Rabbi Isaac N. Trainin, Director of the Commission on Synagogue Relations in New York City, as its chairman. Recently, this committee made a grant of $10,000 to a social agency of black and white Jews, which does work among black Jewish families.

Jim Crow

The term *Jim Crow* is the name of an old Negro song dating back to 1838. It was the first used circa 1861 to designate a railroad car set aside for Negroes and not until 1903 did it come to mean any discriminatory or restrictive measure designed to prevent intermingling on equal terms in public places.

◆

The first Jim Crow law in the South was enacted in Mississippi in 1865. The law, approved by the governor of the state in November, 1865, simply gave legality to a practice which the railroads had already adopted. According to its provisions, it became unlawful for an employee of any railroad in the state to allow "any freedman, negro, or mulatto, to ride in any first class passenger cars, set apart, or used by, and for white persons. . . ." The law was not to apply to Negroes traveling with their mistresses in the capacity of nurses. Although the law applied only to railroads, the principle that it recognized was followed on passenger boats, in theaters, and in a number of other places of public entertainment.

Judges

The nation's first Negro jurist was Judge J. J. Wright, a native of Pennsylvania, who sat for seven years (1870–77) on the Supreme Court of South Carolina. No other Negro rose to such a high judicial post during the whole of the Reconstruction era. Wright was elected to fill out the few months left from the term of

Solomon L. Hodge who had resigned to run for Congress. In the latter part of 1870, Wright was elected for a full six-year term. Wright's decisions showed considerable ability, and his conduct as an associate justice in the turbulent politics of South Carolina demonstrated high integrity.

Born in Pennsylvania in 1840, Wright was the first Negro to be admitted to the bar in that state.

◆

The nation's first Negro municipal judge was Judge Mifflin Gibbs who served as city judge in Little Rock, Arkansas, in 1873. Gibbs had obtained a law degree from Oberlin College in Ohio.

◆

The first Negro federal judge in U.S. history was Judge William Henry Hastie. He was appointed by President Franklin D. Roosevelt judge of the district court of the Virgin Islands and was sworn in in 1937. He served with distinction until 1939, at which time he resigned to become dean and professor of law at the Howard University Law School.

Hastie was born in Knoxville, Tennessee, on November 17, 1904. First in his class and Phi Beta Kappa from Amherst in 1925, he received his LL.B. from Harvard University Law School in 1930, but continued work on an advanced degree, a doctorate in juridical science, which he received from Harvard in 1933.

Hastie left Howard in 1940, in order to accept the job of civilian aide and advisor on race relations to Secretary of War Stimson. Three years later he resigned from this position in the wake of a decision by the army to set up a segregated Air Corps Technical Training School in Missouri. Hastie attributed his quitting to "reactionary policies and discriminatory practices of the Army Air Forces in matters affecting Negroes."

Overnight, Hastie became a national Negro hero. The NAACP awarded him the 1943 Spingarn Medal, annually given to "the American Negro of highest achievement." The citation read:

> William Henry Hastie is selected as the 28th Spingarn Medalist for his distinguished career as jurist and as uncompromising champion of equal justice. As civilian aide to the Secretary of War he refused to temporize with racial bigotry, segregation or discrimination. Men of lesser charac-

ter and of greater selfishness would have closed their eyes to prejudice in order to maintain themselves in a remunerative position. But Judge Hastie refused to do this, resigning in protest against perpetuation of practices which more aptly would have characterized the racial ideology of a dictatorship than of a democracy.

◆

The nation's first Negro woman judge was Judge Jane Matilda Bolin, Yale Law, who was appointed judge of the Court of Domestic Relations on July 22, 1939, by Mayor Fiorello La Guardia of New York City.

◆

The first Negro judge of a United States Customs Court was Judge Irving Charles Mollison of Chicago, Illinois. In 1945, President Harry S Truman appointed Mollison Judge of the United States Customs Court of New York City.

Born in Vicksburg, Mississippi, on December 24, 1898, he received his early education there before going on, first to Oberlin College, and, later, to the University of Chicago. In 1920, having graduated with highest honors, he was awarded a Ph.D. degree and, three years later, a J.D. Shortly thereafter, he was admitted to the Illinois bar and embarked on what proved to be a highly successful law career.

His community activities were many and varied. From 1938 to 1944 he was a director of the Chicago Public Library, after which he served for eighteen months as a member of the board of education. He belonged to several bar associations, was a member of the American Judiciary Society, and served as vice president of the National Urban League. After seventeen years of distinguished service on the bench, Mollison died on May 12, 1962.

◆

The first Negro judge of a U.S. Circuit Court of Appeals was William Henry Hastie, former governor of the Virgin Islands. Hastie was appointed by President Harry S Truman and, on July 19, 1950, unanimously confirmed by the Senate for a recess appointment as Chief Judge to the Third Judicial Circuit (Pennsylvania, New York, Delaware, and the Virgin Islands). He was sworn in by Chief Judge John Biggs, Jr., in Philadelphia, Pennsylvania. The Circuit Court of Appeals ranks second only to the U.S.

Supreme Court in the federal court system. Judge Hastie retired on June 1, 1971, after twenty-one years of service.

◆

The first Negro ever appointed a lifetime federal district judge within the continental United States was Judge Benton Parsons. He was nominated to the U.S. District Court for the Northern District of Illinois by President John F. Kennedy on August 7, 1961. He appeared before the Senate subcommittee on August 17, 1961, and was confirmed by the Senate without a dissenting vote twelve days later. On August 30, he was appointed by President Kennedy and he was installed in office on September 22.

Born in Kansas City, Missouri, on August 13, 1911, Parsons was taken by his parents to Decatur, Illinois, where he spent his childhood. He went to school in Decatur and studied as an undergraduate at James Milikin University and Conservatory of Music. To pay for his schooling, Parsons worked as a composing room helper at the Decatur *Herald Review*.

After he was graduated from Milikin in 1934, he joined the faculty of Lincoln University of Missouri at Jefferson City. From 1938 to 1940, he served as acting head of the department of music at Lincoln University. He attended summer sessions at the University of Wisconsin with an eye toward changing his major to political science. This plan was temporarily interrupted by four years of military service but, with the end of World War II, he pursued his graduate studies, this time at the University of Chicago. He ultimately received an M.A. in political science in 1946, and a Doctor of Laws Degree three years later.

At the 1956 commencement of James Milikin University, Parsons received the merit award of the university for "Distinguished Service in the Field of Jurisprudence."

◆

The first Negro to serve on the highest court of any state since Reconstruction was Otis M. Smith, who was elected to the State Supreme Court of Michigan in November, 1962.

Judge Smith is a man of many "firsts." He was the first Negro to become chairman of the Michigan Public Service Commission. He was appointed to this important post by Governor G. Mennen Williams in 1957. In 1960, he was elected to the office of Auditor General of Michigan, the first Negro to be elected to full-time statewide office since Reconstruction. Another black "first," insofar as the University of Michigan is concerned, was the appointment by Governor Romney of Mr. Smith to a constitutional office, Regent of the University of Michigan.

◆

The first Negro to become a trial examiner in the federal government was Arthur Christopher, Jr., who was appointed in November, 1964, to the staff of the National Labor Relations Board. His job was that of an administrative judge who presided over matters involving unfair labor practices initiated by private individuals, employees, unions, or employers.

Born in September, 1913, Christopher attended high school in his native Jacksonville, Florida. He later received a B.A. from Howard University in Washington, D.C., and an LL.B. in 1944.

◆

The first Negro federal judge to be assigned to preside in courts in the Deep South was Judge L. Watson of New York. He was appointed a U.S. Customs judge in January, 1966. His duties took him into the courtrooms of Texas, Georgia, and Florida.

◆

The first Negro woman to become a federal judge was Mrs. Constance Baker Motley. She was nominated by President Lyndon B. Johnson in February, 1966, to the U.S. District Court for Southern New York. The Senate confirmed President Johnson's nomination of Mrs. Motley.

She was also the first Negro woman ever elected to the New York State Senate and the first woman to be elected borough president of Manhattan.

Born in New Haven, Connecticut, of West Indian parents, Mrs. Motley graduated from New York University and the Columbia University Law School.

Since 1946, Mrs. Motley has been active in all the major school segregation cases initiated by the NAACP Legal Defense Fund. She represented James Meredith, the first Negro to be enrolled in the University of Mississippi; Harvey Gant, the first to enter Clemson College in South Carolina; and led legal teams that desegregated the universities of Alabama, Georgia, and Florida. She was also counsel to Dr. Martin Luther King, Jr., executive

director of the Southern Christian Leadership Conference, in a
number of cases.

◆

The first Negro ever to sit on the U.S. Supreme Court was
Solicitor General Thurgood Marshall, who was chosen by President
Lyndon B. Johnson to succeed Justice Tom C. Clark on June 12,
1967.

"I believe it is the right thing to do, the right time to do it, the
right man and the right place," Johnson said in personally making
the announcement to newsmen summoned to the White House rose
garden.

Marshall was born in Baltimore, Maryland, on July 2, 1908.
After receiving a B.A. degree from Lincoln University as a
predental student, he decided instead to become a lawyer and was
admitted to Howard University's law school, graduating in 1933 at
the top of his class.

After five years of private practice in Baltimore, Marshall
began what was to become a long and distinguished career of
twenty-four years as the chief counsel of the NAACP. He had
presented a number of civil rights cases before the U.S. Supreme
Court, such as the Texas Primary case in 1944, the Restrictive
Covenant cases in 1948, and the now-historic Supreme Court
decision on school desegregation in 1954.

His outstanding achievements in the field of law led, in 1946,
to Marshall's winning the coveted Spingarn Medal, only one of the
numerous citations he holds.

◆

The first Negro to win a judgeship by popular election in the
South since Reconstruction, according to the Voter Education
Project (an adjunct of the Southern Regional Council) was Mrs.
Elireta M. Alexander of Greensboro, North Carolina. She received
her early education in a two-room school run by her Baptist
minister father and her schoolteacher mother. She finished high
school at fifteen and graduated from Greensboro's Agricultural and
Technical University at eighteen. After taking her law degree from
Columbia University, Mrs. Alexander returned to Greensboro and
entered law practice. This course of action ultimately led to her
becoming, in November, 1968, the first Negro judge by election in
the South during this century.

Juries

The first integrated jury in the United States was impaneled to try Jefferson Davis, the president of the Confederacy. Although he had been held in prison since his capture, Davis was released without trial shortly after the impaneling had been made.

Labor

The first attempt to organize an independent national labor convention of Negroes was made in Washington, D.C., in January, 1869. One hundred and thirty delegates were in attendance. This meeting was known as the National Labor Convention of Colored Men. Annual meetings were held in succeeding years but had no effect upon the economic status of the Negro workers. While the meetings were known as labor conventions, most of the time was spent on the discussion topics which, although central to the interests of Negroes, were only incidentally related to labor questions. The activities of labor leaders such as Isaac Myers of the Colored Caulkers Trade Union Society and H. H. Butler of the Colored Engineers' Association were overshadowed by the political presentations of Frederick Douglass and John M. Langston. Political leadership soon replaced labor leadership, and these organizations lost their value as labor units.

◆

The name of the first labor organization of importance, the American Federation of Labor, was adopted on December 8, 1886, at the suggestion of Jeremiah Grandison, a Negro representative at the group's convention.

◆

The first person to introduce a bill founding Labor Day was John Greene, a Negro member of the Ohio Legislature from 1886 to 1890. Labor Day later became a national holiday.

◆

The first Negro vice-president of the AFL-CIO was Asa Philip Randolph, President of the International Brotherhood of Sleeping Car Porters, the strongest labor group among Negroes. With the Pullman car porters as a foundation, Randolph rose to the topmost hierarchy of the labor movement to become, in 1955, the first and only Negro vice-president of the powerful AFL-CIO. He is also the founder and organizer of the American Labor Council. For over forty years, Randolph has hammered away at racial discrimination and segregation. This elder statesman of Negro labor leaders is regarded as a modern-day Moses who was sent to lead his people out of bondage.

During World War II, Randolph threatened to stage a march on Washington in protest against discriminatory practices in the defense establishment and eventually helped persuade President Franklin D. Roosevelt to issue an executive order eliminating such practices. Later, Randolph was an effective lobbyist for the establishment of a fair employment practices committee.

Born in Crescent City, Florida, in 1889, Randolph's education included attendance at Cookman Institute (later Bethune-Cookman College) in Daytona Beach, Florida, and the City College of New York.

◆

The first Negro to serve as a member of the National Labor Relations Board (NLRB) was Howard Jenkins, Jr. He was appointed to a five-year term in 1963 by President John F. Kennedy. The NLRB is the independent federal agency that administers the nation's labor relations laws. Jenkins' services have been praiseworthy.

Jenkins was born in Denver, Colorado, in 1915. He attended the University of Denver and obtained his A.B. degree in 1936. After working nights in the Denver post office, he became the first Negro to obtain an LL.B. degree from the University of Denver. He was also the first Negro to pass the Colorado bar examination.

During World War II, Jenkins held jobs as enforcement officer for the Office of Price Administration and as acting attorney for the War Labor Board in Denver. At the termination of the war, he joined the National Wage Stabilization Office in Denver.

From 1946 to 1956, Jenkins taught labor and administrative law at Howard University and prepared briefs for the Supreme Court and courts of appeal on cases involving the constitutionality of federal and state administrative regulations. During this period, he also did graduate work in law at New York University.

In 1956, Jenkins joined the Department of Labor as an attorney responsible for administrative legal services. After serving one year, he became special assistant to the Solicitor of Labor in the field of international labor affairs. He worked from 1959 to 1962 as director of the Office of Regulations in the Bureau of Labor Management Reports and, from 1962 to 1963, as assistant commissioner in the same bureau.

Law

The first Negro lawyer formally admitted to the bar was Macon B. Allen, who passed his legal examination in Worcester, Massachusetts, and was admitted on May 3, 1845. He had practiced for two years previously in Maine, where no license was required.

◆

The first Negro lawyer to practice before the United States Supreme Court was John S. Rock, who was admitted to practice on February 1, 1865. His admittance was moved by Senator Charles Sumner of Massachusetts.

◆

The first Negro to be admitted to the bar in Pennsylvania was Jonathan Jasper Wright, who was admitted to the bar in that state in 1866. After some college training in Ithaca, New York, Wright studied law in a private office in Pennsylvania.

◆

The first Negro to pass the bar in Illinois was Lloyd G. Wheeler. In 1869, he collected a few law books, sent out news of his business venture by word-of-mouth, and hung out his shingle at 69 West Monroe Street in Chicago. *The Legal News,* a lawyer's publication, welcomed the new barrister by noting: "Mr. Wheeler is an intelligent and worthy gentleman, an honor to his race, and no disgrace to the bar of Illinois. . . . We wish him success."

Wheeler died on September 8, 1909, at Tuskegee, Alabama.

◆

The first Negro woman to graduate from a university law school in the United States was Charlotte E. Ray, who received an LL.B. degree from the School of Law at Howard University. She was admitted to the Supreme Court of the District of Columbia on April 23, 1872.

◆

The first Negro lawyer to be admitted to the bar in Georgia was John F. Quarles of Atlanta, who passed a "creditable examination" in 1873.

◆

The first Negro to be admitted to the bar in Florida was James Weldon Johnson, the writer and educator, who was born in Jacksonville, Florida, in 1871. After finishing grade school, Johnson went to Atlanta University for secondary and college education and compiled an enviable all-around record as campus leader, football and baseball star, honor student, and member of the college quartet which toured New England to raise funds for the school.

After graduating from Atlanta University in 1894, Johnson returned to Jacksonville and became principal of the Stanton School, a grade school to which he added a high school department. In 1897, he completed his legal studies and became the first Negro to be admitted to the Florida bar through examination in the state court.

Johnson attained his fame, of course, in the field of poetry rather than in that of law.

◆

The first major association of Negro lawyers was the National Bar Association (NBA). Founded in 1925, the Association now has approximately 2,500 members.

◆

The first Negro woman lawyer to practice before the U.S. Supreme Court was Violette Neatly Anderson of Chicago, Illinois, who was admitted on January 29, 1926.

◆

The first Negro to pass the Colorado bar examination was Howard Jenkins, Jr., of Denver, Colorado.

Born on June 16, 1915, Jenkins received his B.A. from the University of Denver in 1936, and soon thereafter became the first Negro to receive an LL.B. from the same institution.

◆

The first Negro to be named editor in chief of the *North*

Carolina Law Review was Julius LeVonne Chambers, who received this honor in 1961. This is the highest honor at the University of North Carolina Law School. Chambers, one of the four Negroes in the 314-student law school, was top man scholastically in his class of one hundred. He had an A average. When asked about Chambers' race, Dean Henry Brandis, Jr., said: "I have had my statement prepared for a long while. It is just three words—he earned it." Chambers commented: "I don't look upon myself as any sort of star or shining example. But I would hope that anything I achieved could be shown as proof to others of my race as well as the white race that Negroes can achieve these things."

◆

The first Negro dean of a predominantly white law school in the nation was Ronald Davenport, who was appointed dean of the law school of Duquesne University in April, 1970, at the age of thirty-three. A native of Philadelphia, Davenport began his legal experience as a clerk with a Philadelphia law firm.

Attorney Davenport received a B.S. in economics from the University of Pennsylvania, the LL.B. from Temple University School of Law, and the LL.M. at Yale University Law School. He joined the Duquesne law school faculty in 1963 as an assistant professor, advanced to associate professor, and, since 1967, has been a full professor of law.

Mr. Davenport, also the president of the Urban League of Pittsburgh, won the Francis Keller Prize at Yale for a paper on international law and received his master's degree there in 1963. At Temple he received the Robert E. Lamberton Award for the highest grade in constitutional law and the Nat N. Wolfsohn Memorial Award for the highest grade in real property. He graduated in 1962.

◆

The first known Negro to head a predominantly white local or state bar group is attorney W. Henry Walker, who was elected president of the sixty-five-member East Chicago (Indiana) Bar Association for a two-year term in 1970. A well-known Democrat, Walker was close to both the Kennedy and Johnson administrations. In his new position, Walker took over an organization that has three black lawyers.

◆

The first Negro admitted to practice before the Supreme Court of Pennsylvania was T. Morris Chester. He was admitted in 1851.

In 1866, Mr. Chester visited Europe and passed the winter in Russia; he was cordially received at the courts of Denmark, Sweden, Saxony, and England. After spending four years in Europe, Mr. Chester studied law at Middle Temple Inn, London, and was admitted to the English bar in 1870, thus becoming the first Negro lawyer in England.

He returned to America in 1871, and settled in New Orleans, Louisiana, where he practiced law and was prominent in the establishment of schools for the education of his race. At the same time, he was placed in command of the First Brigade of the Louisiana Guard. In 1873, he was appointed U.S. Commissioner, serving until 1879. In 1884, he became president of the Willmington Wrightville and Onslow Railroad.

Libraries

The first known Negro founder of a public library was Amos Fortune, who became one of the founders of the Jaffrey Public Library in Jaffrey, New Hampshire, in 1795.

Amos Fortune was born about 1710 in Africa and was brought to this country as a slave. In 1769, he purchased his freedom in Massachusetts. Nine years later he was able to buy freedom for his wife Violet Baldwin, and his adopted daughter, Celyndia.

In 1781, Amos Fortune, then about seventy years of age, moved to Jaffrey to establish himself as a tanner, employing both black and white apprentices.

Each year during the summer, the Amos Fortune Forum is held as a memorial in the Old Meeting House where the ex-slave attended church services. Both Fortune and his wife lie in the meeting house burial ground.

Governor Lane Dwinell of New Hampshire issued a proclamation in 1955 declaring: "Now therefore I, Lane Dwinell, Governor of the State of New Hampshire, in behalf of our people do proclaim the day February 20, 1955 to be Amos Fortune Day and I do call upon the citizens of New Hampshire to consider on that day their obligations of tolerance and good citizenship."

The first known Negro to attain a professional position in the Library of Congress was Daniel Murray, who served as a member of the staff in various capacities "up to an assistant librarian," from 1871 to 1922.

Daniel Murray was born in Baltimore, March 3, 1851. His parents were free and fully alive to the benefits of education and though their circumstances were limited, they were able to give Daniel every educational advantage possible in a slaveholding state. When about five years old he was allowed to go to a small primary school in the neighborhood taught by Miss Catherine Young. Later teachers were Charles C. Fortie, a noted schoolteacher in Baltimore; Alfred Handy; W. H. Hunter; James Lynch, who became Congressman from Mississippi; and Reverend George T. Watkins. Finally Murray attended the Unitarian Seminary in Baltimore.

The Preliminary List of Books and Pamphlets by Negro Authors, for Paris Exposition and Library of Congress (1900), compiled by Daniel Murray, appears to have been the first effort on the part of the library of Congress to draw attention to the works by and about Negroes.

Murray died in 1923.

◆

The first time a major public library devoted one of its branches exclusively to the study and collection of materials on the Negro was the formation of the Schomburg Collection in the Harlem Branch of the New York City Public Library. In 1926, the Carnegie Corporation bought the collection of Arthur A. Schomburg, a Puerto Rican of African descent, and presented it to the New York Public Library. Since then, the collection has grown to more than 43,000 books, bound periodicals, and pamphlets, 4,000 manuscripts, 200 scrapbooks and news clippings, 1,032 microfilm reels (mostly of 400 different Negro newspapers), and 140 pieces of African art. The library is one of the nation's most important reference centers for the study of Negro life and history. The purpose of the Schomburg Collection, Mrs. Jean Hutson, Curator, points out, is to amass, preserve, and organize all significant materials about peoples of African descent, and to keep this record up-to-date and available to the public.

◆

The first Negro to head a major library system in the country is Mrs. Clara Jones, fifty-six, who was elected director of the Detroit Public Library in 1970.

Literature

The first Negro to write poetry in America is generally considered to be Lucy Terry. In a ballad which she called "Bars Fight," she recreated an Indian massacre which occurred in Deersfield, Massachusetts, in 1746, during King George's War. Although of little poetic value, "Bars Fight" has been hailed by one historian as "the best and most colorful version extant."

Mrs. Terry's birthplace is not known, but she was living in Deersfield, Massachusetts, a slave of Ensign Ebenezer Wells, at the time of the bloody Indian raid on the settlers of that town on August 25, 1746.

After her marriage to a free Negro named Prince (as a slave she was not permitted to take the surname of her husband), she is said to have built up an enviable reputation as a storyteller. Her home became a community center for young people who enjoyed listening to her tales.

Eventually Lucy acquired a reputation as a speaker and once used her eloquence in a three-hour attempt to persuade the Board of Trustees of Williams College to permit her son to enter the school. Apparently this attempt met with success.

The following lines are from her poem:

> August 'twas the twenty fifth
> Seventeen hundred forty-six
> The Indians did in ambush lay
> Some very valient men to slay
> The names of whom I'll not leave out
> Samuel Allen like a hero fout
> And though he was so brace and bold
> His face no more shall we behold
> Eleazer Hawks was killed outright
> Before he had time to fight
> Before he did the Indians see
> Was shot and killed immediately . . .

The first Negro to publish poems in America was **Jupiter Hammon**, a slave belonging to a Mr. Lloyd of Queens Village,

Long Island. His first poem appeared in 1760, and was entitled, "An Evening Thought, Salvation by Christ, with Penitential Cries."

Due to his fondness for preaching, the major portion of Hammon's poetry is religious in tone. One of his best-known works is, however, a prose piece entitled, "An Address to the Negroes of the State of New York City," which was made on September 24, 1786. The speech was published the following year and eventually went into the collection of J. Pierpont Morgan.

The first American Negro poet to publish a volume of verse was Phillis Wheatley. Her original volume entitled *Poems on Various Subjects, Religious,* was published in 1773 in Algate, London. Although her poetry was as good as the best being written in America, it was largely imitative. It is considered important today largely because of its historical role in the growth of American Negro literature.

Born in Senegal in 1753, Phillis was brought to the United States as a slave, and received her name from Mrs. Susannah Wheatley, the wife of the Boston tailor who had bought her on the Boston slave block in 1761. She received her early education in the household of her master. Her interest in writing stemmed from reading the Bible and the classics under the guidance of the Wheatley's daughter Mary.

When the Revolution erupted, Phillis wrote George Washington a complimentary poem upon his appointment to head the colonial armies. He replied: "I thank you most sincerely for your polite notice of me in the elegant lines you enclosed, and however undeserving I may be of such encomium and panegyric, the style and manner exhibit a striking proof of your poetical talents."

In 1794, Phillis' last poem, "Liberty and Peace," was published. She died during the same year at the age of forty.

The first Negro autobiography was by Richard Allen, first bishop of the African Methodist Episcopal Church. Published in 1793, it was the first in a long series of personal narratives by distinguished Negroes.

The first collection of Negro poetry in America was *Les Cenelles,* which was published in 1845 by Armand Lanusse, a freeborn New Orleans Negro. Lanusse contributed some of his own poems to the anthology, which contained some eighty-two poems in all.

◆

The first Negro in America to write a novel was William Wells Brown. He wrote *Clotel,* a narrative of slave life in the United States, the story of an efficient colored woman represented as the housekeeper of Thomas Jefferson. In the novel one of the woman's two daughters drowns herself in the Potomac River to elude pursuing slavers. The book was first published in London, England, in 1853, and reprinted with slight changes in 1864, in Boston, Massachusetts, under the title, *Clotelle, A Call of the Southern States.* It contained 104 pages and sold for ten cents.

Brown was born a slave in Lexington, Kentucky, in 1815. He was taken to St. Louis as a young boy. His education came from an apprenticeship to the antislavery editor Elijah P. Lovejoy of the *St. Louis Times.* In 1834, Brown fled to Canada. As author of a novel, a drama, and a travel book, he was the first American Negro to write books in three different genres.

Brown was also one of our first Negro historians. His historical studies include *The Black Man: His Antecedents, His Genius, and His Achievements* (1863), *The Negro in the American Revolution: His Heroism and Fidelity* (1867), and *The Rising Sun* (1874). Brown died in 1888.

◆

The first Negro woman to have a novel published was Frances Ellen Harper, abolitionist, poet, and lecturer. Her book, *Iola Leroy: The Shadows Lifted,* was released in 1860. Her other published works include *Moses: A Story of the Nile; The Dying Bondsman: Eliza Crossing the Ice; Poems;* and *Sketches of Southern Life.* Her best-known poem is "Bury Me in a Free Land."

◆

The first nationally known Negro poet in the United States was Paul Laurence Dunbar, born in 1872 of ex-slave parentage in Dayton, Ohio, where he was the only black student in his high school graduating class.

While Dunbar wrote several novels during his short life, including *The Uncalled* (1898) and *The Love of Landry* (1900), he is best known for his poems, which led William Dean Howells to describe him as the first American Negro "to feel the Negro life aesthetically and express it lyrically." His *Oak and Ivy* (1893), *Majors and Minors* (1896), and *Lyrics of Lowly Life* (1896) have caused many critics to refer to him as the "poet laureate of the Negro race."

At the Negro Pavilion of the 1893 World's Fair in Chicago, Dunbar worked as an assistant to Frederick Douglass and read his poems. During Queen Victoria's Diamond Jubilee, he went to London to recite his work. In that era, when the poems of Robert Burns, Eugene Fields, and others were popular, the simple musical dialect verses of Dunbar also achieved a wide audience, especially his humorous poems in the quaint broken English of the newly freed Negroes.

"In Dunbar's time," wrote Benjamin G. Brawley, "black was not fashionable. The burden still rested upon the Negro to prove that he could do what any other man could do, and in America that meant to use the white man's technique and meet the white man's standard of excellence . . . This was the test . . . he had to satisfy, and not many will doubt that he met it admirably."

Dunbar's poems went through many editions, and before he died in 1906, he was one of America's famous men of letters.

◆

The first organization of artistic and scholarly blacks was the American Negro Academy, established in March, 1897. The first president and leader of the academy was Alexander Crummell, an Episcopal clergyman, who was born on March 3, 1819, and died in 1898. He graduated from Queens College at Cambridge in England in 1853, with the degree of Bachelor of Arts.

Associated with Crummell were Francis J. Grimke, a Presbyterian minister, and his brother, Archibald Grimke, an attorney, both graduates of Lincoln University, the former also a graduate of Princeton Theological Seminary and the latter also one of the Harvard Law School; Lewis B. Moore, a graduate of the University of Pennsylvania and Kelley Miller, a graduate of Howard University and Johns Hopkins University, both deans at Howard; J. Albert Johnson, a Canadian Medical School graduate and later an A.M.E. bishop; W. E. B. Du Bois, a Fisk and Harvard graduate and later an educator and writer; William S. Scarborough, a graduate of Atlanta University and Oberlin, and later president of Wilberforce University; John W. Cromwell, historian and newspaper editor; and William H. Crogman, president of Clark University.

The objects of the first academy were "the promotion of literature, science and art, the fostering of higher education, the publication of scholarly work and the defense of the Negro against vicious assault." This academy terminated in 1916.

There were few organizations in black life and history with the scholarly ideals enunciated by this first academy, until the rise of the Black Academy of Arts and Letters, founded in Boston in 1969. This academy was incorporated in New York as a nonprofit corporation whose purpose it is "to define, reserve, cultivate, promote, foster and develop the arts and letters of black people."

◆

The Negro in Literature and Art by Benjamin Brawley (1918) was the first book devoted exclusively to this aspect of Negro history. It undertakes "to treat somewhat more thoroughly than has ever before been attempted the achievement of the Negro in the United States along literary and artistic lines, judging this by absolute rather than by partial or limited standards."

◆

The first Negro detective novel was written by Rudolph Fisher. Entitled *The Conjure-Man Dies,* the book was published in 1932.

◆

The first Negro poet to be employed to teach creative writing by a Negro university was James Weldon Johnson. He was appointed in January, 1932, by Fisk University in Nashville, Tennessee, to the Adam K. Spence Chair of Creative Literature and Writing, founded in memory of a Fisk professor who taught these subjects. In 1934 Johnson was asked to become a visiting professor of literature at New York University.

James Weldon Johnson has been called "the only true artist among the early Negro novelists." In his early days, Johnson's fame rested largely on his work as a lyricist for popular songs but in 1917 he completed his first book of poetry, *Fifty Years and Other Poems*. His *Autobiography of an Ex-Colored Man* (1912) is one of the earliest accounts of a Negro exploring different levels of American society by "passing." In 1937, Johnson enhanced his literary reputation with *God's Trombones,* a collection of seven folk sermons in verse. His poem "O Black and Unknown Bards," appearing in a collection of his verse entitled *St. Peter Relates an Incident,* is still accepted as the best poetic explanation of the origins of the Negro spirituals. His lengthy autobiography, *Along This Way,* was published in 1930.

Johnson died in 1938, following an automobile accident in Maine.

◆

The first book to tell the story of the Reconstruction era from the Negro's viewpoint was written by Dr. W. E. B. Du Bois. His book *Black Reconstruction* was published in 1935. For sixty years historians had been describing the Reconstruction period as the "tragic era." Du Bois saw Reconstruction as a time of true democracy in the South. The "tragedy" came when this democracy was crushed and Negroes were deprived of their rights. Other book written by Dr. Du Bois were *The Gift of Black Folk, Darkwater, The Quest of the Silver Fleece, Dark Princess, Black Folk Now and Then, Dusk of Dawn, The Negro Souls of Black Folk, John Brown, The World and Africa, Ordeal of Mansart,* and *Autobiography of W. E. B. Du Bois.* He edited the introductory volume of *Encyclopedia of the Negro* and started a scholarly magazine, *Phylon* (from a Greek word meaning "race").

◆

Dr. W. E. B. Du Bois, writer, and educator, was the first Negro elected to the National Institute of Arts and Letters. His election occurred on December 22, 1943.

◆

The first Negro to win the Pulitzer Prize was Gwendolyn Brooks. She received this prestigious award in 1950 for *Annie Allen,* a volume of her poetry which had been published a year earlier.

Eighteen years later, after the death of poet Carl Sandburg, Miss Brooks became Illinois' poet laureate. That honor, too, marked a first for her race.

Miss Brooks was born in Topeka, Kansas, on June 7, 1917. She moved to Chicago at an early age and attended Wilson Junior College, where she majored in literature, graduating in 1936. This was the termination of her formal education.

Her work first began to attract attention in 1943 and 1944, when she won the Poetry Workshop Award at the Midwestern Writers Conference held at Northwestern University.

In 1945, Miss Brooks completed a book of poems, *A Street in Bronzeville,* and was selected by *Mademoiselle* magazine as one of the year's ten most outstanding American women. In 1946, she was also a Guggenheim Fellow in creative writing. In 1949, she won the Eunice Tietjen Prize for Poetry in the annual competition sponsored by *Poetry* magazine.

Her other books include a collection of children's poems, *Bronzeville Boys and Girls* (1956), *Maud Martha* (1953), and two books of poetry, *The Bean Eaters* (1960) and *Selected Poems* (1963).

Currently, Miss Brooks is a faculty member at Northeastern College.

See also Almanacs; Drama; History.

Lynching

The first serious statistical treatment of the tragedy of lynching was written by Ida Bell Wells, a Negro, and the pioneer of the antilynching crusade in the United States. Her study of lynching, written in 1895, was entitled *The Red Record*. She appealed to President William McKinley for support in the fight against lynch law. She said that "nowhere in the civilized world save the United States, do men go out in bands of fifty to 5,000, to hunt down, shoot, hang or burn to death, a single individual, unarmed and absolutely powerless."

Miss Wells was born in Holly Springs, Mississippi, on July 18, 1862, and was orphaned at fourteen, but managed to attend Rust College and Fisk University. After a few courses at Fisk, she went to work as a school teacher in Memphis, and began writing about the inferior conditions of black schools; as a result, she lost her teaching position. Following this incident, she took her life savings and opened a small newspaper, which she called *Free Speech*.

Through this newspaper she continued her attacks on lynching and its attendant evils. Her press was soon destroyed, and she was driven out of Memphis for her antilynching zeal. She relocated in Chicago and there joined Jane Addams and other humanitarians in a number of liberal causes. Miss Wells traveled to other large cities in the East and in Europe to speak out against lynching.

The Woman's Loyal Union financed a lecture tour for her in Great Britain, and her lectures caused such a great outcry against lynchings in Britain that a British clergyman said, "Nothing since the days of *Uncle Tom's Cabin* had taken such a hold in England as the antilynching crusade."

Using Chicago as her headquarters, Miss Wells helped found the NAACP in 1910; helped organize antilynching societies all over the United States and one in England; became known as the mother of Negro women's clubs; fought for women's suffrage; helped curb the establishment of separate schools in Chicago; served as the city's first Negro adult probation officer; helped found the Wabash YMCA; and led the fight for Chicago's first Negro alderman and congressman.

Later, through marriage, Miss Wells became Mrs. Barnett. She died in Chicago on March 1, 1931. On October 27, 1940, a huge Chicago Housing Authority low-rent project carrying her name was dedicated.

◆

The congressman to introduce the first bill making lynching a federal offense was George H. White, a Negro from North Carolina, who served two terms in Congress, from 1897 to 1901. White became a vigorous defender of Negro rights. In one of his most important addresses from the floor, he made an impassioned attack on lynching and mob law: ". . . We have struggled on as best we could with the odds against us at every turn. Our constitutional rights have been trodden under foot; . . . fully 50,000 of my race have been ignominiously murdered by mobs, not one percent of whom have been made to answer for their crimes in the courts of justice, and even here in the nation's Capital—in the Senate and House—Senators and Representatives have undertaken the unholy task of extenuating and excusing these foul deeds, and in some instances they have gone so far as to justify them."

Such speeches incurred the wrath of White's fellow congressmen, but he continued his strong stand against lynching and other forms of injustice to Negroes. To the relief of many congressmen, he left Congress in 1901, the last Negro to serve in that body until Oscar DePriest was elected from Illinois in 1928.

Magazines

The first Negro magazine appeared in America in 1841, in Philadelphia; it was edited by George Hogarth and published by the African Methodist Episcopal Church. It was called the *Review.* The magazine was interested in the broad problems of human and moral brotherhood. The foreword to the first issue, after observing that the General Conference of the Church had long hesitated such a magazine because of fear of failure, optimistically explained that "times have changed in our favor as a people, light has burst forth upon us, intelligence in a great measure is taking the place of ignorance, especially among the younger people, opening the avenues to proper Christian feeling and benevolence. . . ."

◆

The first weekly Negro magazine, *Jet,* was introduced to the public in November, 1951, by John H. Johnson. *Jet* is a pocket-sized news and picture magazine with an up-to-the-minute summary of the most significant news involving Negroes, as well as features on leading personalities. *Jet* now sells over 400,000 copies a week.

Other popular Negro magazines published by Johnson Publishing Company, Inc., are *Ebony, Tan,* and *Negro Digest.*

Mathematics

The first known Negro mathematician in the United States was Benjamin Banneker. Born in 1731, in Maryland, he was educated in a private school with whites. W. E. B. Du Bois observed of Banneker: "He became an expert in the solution of difficult mathematical problems, corresponding with interested persons of leisure." Banneker was also an astronomer and an inventor of note.

◆

The first Negro to receive a Ph.D. in mathematics was Elbert Cox, who received this degree in 1925 from Cornell University.

The first Negro teenager to receive a Ph.D. was J. Ernest Wilkins, Jr. Ex-prodigy Ernest, a Phi Beta Kappa, earned a Ph.D. in mathematics from the University of Chicago at the age of nineteen. Dr. Wilkins is currently working as an atomic scientist with the Nuclear Development Corporation of America in White Plains, New York.

Mayors

The first Negro mayor of a biracial Mississippi city was Robert H. Wood, who served as mayor of historic Natchez during the Reconstruction period. Mayor Wood may well be the first black mayor in the history of America.

The first Negro mayor of Flint, Michigan—the second largest city in the state—was Floyd J. McCree, who took office in 1966.

The first Negro mayor of Springfield, Ohio, Robert C. Henry, took office in 1966.

The first Negro taking office as mayor of the capital of the United States in ninety-three years was Walter Washington of Washington, D.C. Present at his swearing-in ceremony on September 28, 1967, were Associate Justice Abe Fortas of the Supreme Court, who administered the oath; Thomas Fletcher, deputy mayor; and President and Mrs. Lyndon B. Johnson. Mayor Washington was appointed by President Johnson.

The first Negro to be elected mayor of a major American city was Carl Stokes, who was elected Mayor of Cleveland, Ohio, in November, 1967. With a staggering ninety-five percent of the city's Negro vote, and forty-three thousand white ballots as well, the handsome great-grandson of a slave defeated the grandson of President William Howard Taft for the mayoralty. The Negro population of Cleveland—the eighth most populous city in the United States—is thirty-five percent.

Stokes had been an attorney in a law firm with his brother. He was elected in 1962 to the Ohio legislature as the first Negro Democrat in that body. Regarded by many as a diligent and effective member of the Ohio House of Representatives, he was re-elected for two terms. He resigned from this position upon his election as Cleveland's mayor.

◆

Another first Negro mayor of a major American city elected in 1967 was Richard Gordon Hatcher, who became mayor of Gary, Indiana, the second largest city in Indiana, and one of the important urban industrial centers of the nation.

Hatcher earned his law degree from Valparaiso University in 1959. The following year he came to Gary, where he served as deputy prosecutor in Lake County Criminal Court before being elected mayor.

◆

The first Negro to be elected mayor in a predominantly white Southern community was Howard Nathaniel Lee, who was elected mayor of Chapel Hill, North Carolina, in May, 1969. He was chosen by 2,567 votes out of a record 4,734 cast. Former Vice-President Hubert Humphrey commented in a congratulatory telegram: "This is a new breakthrough in Southern politics."

Lee is the son of a Georgia sharecropper, a child of the Depression, who was twice a high school dropout. He eventually went to Georgia's Fort Valley State College, worked as a probation officer in Savannah, and then moved to Chapel Hill in 1964, and took a master's degree in social work at the University of North Carolina in 1966. He worked as an employee relations counselor at nearby Duke University. Lee's strenuous campaign centered on the contention that Chapel Hill (population: 12,500), whose voting population is less than ten percent Negro, was failing to meet the needs of its people in public transportation, recreation, city planning, and housing. Lee swept the town's black vote but drew his basic support among whites from the liberal University of North Carolina community that had supported Senator Eugene McCarthy for president in the 1968 Democratic primary.

North Carolina is the South's most liberal state, and Chapel Hill has long had an envied reputation as one of its most liberal towns. As long ago as 1961, the University of North Carolina had already become one of the first state schools in Dixie to crack the color barrier, and in the years that followed Chapel Hill took upon itself to develop its own civil rights program without national headlines or police dogs.

◆

The first Negro elected mayor of a biracial city in Mississippi since Reconstruction was Charles Evers, who was elected mayor of Fayette, Mississippi, in July, 1969. Fayette's 1,600 population is about three-to-one Negro.

At his inaugural ball, Evers told an audience of his supporters that he must prove that Negroes can govern without bitterness. "We don't want to do to the white folks what they have done to us," he said. "There will be equal justice; not black justice but equal justice."

Aaron Henry of Clarksdale, state president of the National Association for the Advancement of Colored People, opened the inaugural program with the reading of telegrams. One from President Nixon said: "I want you to know my thoughts are with you. . . ." Former President Lyndon Johnson told Evers that in winning the election "you experienced the thrill of democracy." And former Vice-President Humphrey wired: "I know you will serve with distinction."

Later, Evers (who is the brother of Medgar Evers, a civil rights worker who was killed in the South) observed: "Blacks are shouting 'black power.' But the only powers that whites understand and respond to are vote and green and of the two, vote power is the most powerful."

◆

The first Negro to be elected vice-mayor of Atlanta, Georgia, in its 122-year history was attorney Maynard Jackson. Jackson, thirty-one, a vice president of the Atlanta NAACP who ran on a platform of enforcing antidiscrimination laws, defeated veteran Milton Farris 55,000 to 35,000 in the Georgia capital's first biracial election for mayor and vice-mayor, held in 1969.

◆

The first Negro to be elected mayor of a northeastern city is Kenneth Gibson, who was elected mayor of Newark, New Jersey, in June, 1970.

Gibson was born in Enterprise, Alabama, and moved with his family to the predominantly black south ward of Newark at the age of eight. His first jobs were in factories. Then he enrolled in the evening division at Newark College of Engineering, and twelve years later gained his civil engineering degree.

◆

The first Negro mayor of East St. Louis, Illinois, is James E. Williams, a lawyer who won election on April 6, 1971, by divorcing himself from all organized politics.

Williams, a newcomer to politics, won over another black candidate, Virgil Calvert, the city's building Commissioner, in a nonpartisan runoff.

The city's population of 70,000 is about 70 per cent Negro, and the voter registration of 36,019 is about 50 per cent black. The final count was 10,813 for Williams and 8,202 for Calvert with about half of the registered voters casting ballots.

◆

The first Negro mayor of Berkeley, California, is Warren Widner, who resigned his position on the City Council to run successfully for mayor on April 6, 1971, at the age of 33. The mayor of Berkeley is a voting member of the nine-member City Council, but the mayor's job itself is now largely ceremonial.

Medicine

The first regularly recognized Negro physician in the United States was Dr. James Derham of New Orleans. He was born in 1757, in Philadelphia, where he was taught to read and write, and instructed in the principles of Christianity. With his master, Dr. John Kearsley, Derham learned to compound medicines and to perform some of the more humble acts of attention to his patients. After the death of Dr. Kearsley, Derham was owned by Dr. George West, a British regimental surgeon under whom he progressed further in medical work. He was transferred finally to Dr. Robert Dove at New Orleans, who liberated him on easy terms in recognition of his medical ability. By about 1783, when he was twenty-six years old, he had built a practice in New Orleans estimated at $3,000 annually, and established a reputation as one of the most distinguished physicians in Louisiana. Historian Bousfield has justly called Dr. Derham "the father of Negro doctors in this country." Dr. Benjamin Rush said of Dr. Derham, "I have conversed with him upon most of the acute and epidemic diseases of the country where he lives and was pleased to find him perfectly acquainted with the modern simple mode of practice on these diseases. I expected to have suggested some new medicines to him, but he suggested many more to me."

◆

The first Negro hospital and asylum founded by whites solely for Negroes was chartered on December 24, 1832, as the Georgia Infirmary for the Relief and Protection of Aged and Afflicted Negroes, of Savannah, Georgia. The organizational meeting was held at the Exchange (a mercantile building) on January 15, 1833.

◆

The first American Negro to obtain a formal medical degree was Dr. James McCune Smith of New York. He received the A.B. in 1835, the M.A. in 1846, and the M.D. in 1837—all from the University of Glasgow in Scotland. He returned to New York in 1837, and there he developed a highly successful practice and established two apothecary shops. Dr. Smith devoted a significant portion of his time and energy in combating invidious racial inferiority myths. Hence we find coming from his pen such essays as "Comparative Anatomy of the Races" and "The Influence of Climate on Longevity, with Special Reference to Insurance." He was also a vigorous and able performer on the rostrum, and is said to have bested John C. Calhoun in 1843 in a public debate on the biological capacities of the Negro.

◆

The first Negroes to be graduated from an American medical school were Dr. John V. deGrasse of New York and Thomas J. White of Brooklyn, both of whom received their degrees from Bowdoin College in Maine in 1849. Dr. deGrasse was the first Negro doctor to become a member of a medical association. He was admitted to the Boston Medical Society in 1854, in recognition of his professional ability.

◆

The first seeds of Meharry Medical College, the famous Negro school, were sown on a lonely country trail in Illinois by a Negro freedman.

Early in the nineteenth century, Samuel Meharry, while traveling through southern Illinois with a load of merchandise, presumably salt, drawn by a horse on a wagon, became stuck in the mud and was unable to proceed on his journey. The only sign of habitation in the neighborhood was the cabin of a Negro freedman (whose name has never been discovered). The Negro, seeing his plight, offered Meharry room and board for the night and the next morning helped him out of the mire and saw him on his way. Upon departing, Samuel Meharry told the Negro freedman that he had no money with which to pay him for his kindness but that he would some day do something for his people. Years later when Samuel Meharry had accumulated "some of this world's good" he and his four brothers pooled their resources and made a gift of $35,000 to Central Tennessee College for the establishment of a medical department for the training of freedmen. This was the beginning of Meharry Medical College, which opened in 1876.

◆

The first Negro to obtain the position of surgeon in the United States Army was Dr. Alexander T. Augusta, who qualified by competitive examination. He served during the Civil War period. After the war he became one of the leading Negro physicians in the District of Columbia.

◆

The first Negro woman awarded a medical degree was Rebecca Lee, who received an M.D. degree on March 1, 1864, from the New England Female Medical College in Boston. She completed a seventeen-week course to earn the M.D. degree.

◆

The first Negro medical school in the U.S. was the Howard University Medical School. Howard opened its doors on November 9, 1868, with eight students and five teachers, of whom one, Dr. Alexander T. Augusta, demonstrator of Anatomy, was a Negro. Dr. Augusta, who studied medicine at the University of Toronto, was the first Negro to serve on the faculty of any American medical school. The university had been chartered on March 2, 1867. The stated purpose of the medical department was "to assist (the) agencies already at work in the relief of ignorance and personal suffering in the District of Columbia and in the country at large."

◆

The first Negro dentist in the U.S. to receive a doctor's degree was Dr. Robert T. Freeman. He was born in Washington, D.C. He attended the first class in dentistry at Harvard University and graduated from Harvard in 1869. Dr. Robert C. Weaver, the first Negro to hold a cabinet post in U.S. history, is Freeman's grandson.

◆

The first Negro medical society was the Medico-Chirurgical Society of the District of Columbia, which was organized on April 24, 1884, in Washington, D.C. The first president was Dr. Robert Reyburn.

◆

The first interracial hospital in the United States was the Provident Hospital in Chicago, Illinois, incorporated on January 23, 1891, and opened on May 4, 1891. The structure was located at 29th and Dearborn streets, in the heart of the "Black Belt," as the Negro area was called at that time. Although primarily for Negroes, there was no racial barrier as to the admission of patients or staff appointments of physicians. The stated purpose of the hospital was the "proper care of the sick and injured without regard to race, creed, or color."

When Provident Hospital first opened its doors in a two-story frame house, it was the only hospital in Chicago where black physicians could bring their patients, the only one to train black nurses, and the only private hospital that freely accepted all black patients.

◆

The first Negro medical journal was the *Medical and Surgical Observer,* published in Jackson, Tennessee, in December, 1892. The first issue was 32 pages long. It appeared regularly for eighteen months. The first editor was Dr. Vandahurst Lynk.

◆

The first president and one of the founders of the National Medical Association was Dr. Robert Boyd, who was born in Pulaski, Tennessee, on July 8, 1858. Dr. Boyd was a dentist and a pharmacist as well as a physician, earning all three degrees from Meharry Medical College. Boyd was the first black doctor to practice in Nashville, Tennessee, and was considered one of the top surgeons of his generation. The National Medical Association was organized in 1895, as the black counterpart of the American Medical Association.

◆

The first doctor in the world to perform a successful operation on the human heart was Dr. Daniel Hale Williams, a Negro. He was born in Holidaysburg, Pennsylvania, in 1856. In 1883, he graduated from the medical school of Northwestern University but stayed there as an anatomy instructor for four years.

Dr. Williams' life is a long list of "firsts." He was the first man to introduce a training program for Negro nurses. He was the practical dreamer whose plans led to the founding of the world's first interracial hospital (Provident in Chicago), an institution that served all races in the mixed community in which it was founded. Dr. Williams served on the staff of Provident Hospital. He was the first Negro on the Illinois State Board of Health, and a founder and first vice president of the National Medical Association. He was elected in 1913 as the first Negro Fellow of the American College of Surgeons.

On July 9, 1893, a man was rushed to Provident Hospital with a stab wound in the chest. Dr. Williams opened his chest, found the pericardial sac, emptied it of blood, and successfully sutured it. Almost overnight Dr. Williams brought fame to the hospital and to himself as one of the outstanding surgeons in the world.

Dr. Williams died in 1931 after a lifetime devotion to his two main interests—the NAACP and the construction of hospitals and training schools for Negro doctors and nurses.

◆

The first Negro professor at Harvard University Medical School was Dr. William A. Hinton who became world famous for his development of the "Hinton Test" for syphilis. Dr. Hinton was born in Chicago, and received a B.S. degree from Harvard College in 1905. After teaching for several years in the South, he entered Harvard Medical School, graduating in 1912. His teaching career at the school began the same year, when he became an instructor of preventive medicine; he continued at Harvard until his retirement in 1950. "He taught with devotion and undiminished gusto," a colleague recalled, "and his manner, friendly and informal, invited the student to learn in an atmosphere free of academic protocol."

In 1927, Dr. Hinton developed a new blood test for the detection of syphilis and in further studies he determined and improved its sensitivity and accuracy. The test is still widely used. Later, with Dr. John Davis, Hinton developed a test on spinal fluids for the detection of syphilis. In 1936, he published his authorative textbook, *Syphilis and its Treatment*.

Director of the Massachusetts State Wassermann Laboratory since its establishment in 1915, Hinton was its chief stimulus for more than thirty-eight years, until he relinquished the directorship in 1954. For years this important serologic laboratory was called the "Hinton Laboratory" because of his association with it and because his famous test was and still is the one most commonly used in the state. Here he helped to set up one of the first schools in the United States for training medical technicians. Under his guidance, the Wassermann Laboratory became a model of its kind, and Hinton helped to establish over one hundred new diagnostic laboratories when Massachusetts established prenatal and premarital laws.

At his death in 1959, Dr. Hinton was clinical professor of bacteriology and immunology, emeritus. Massachusetts Governor Christian A. Herter had told Dr. Hinton in an official letter: "Your name is known the world over for singular achievements which have benefited all mankind."

◆

The first black person to be appointed to head a Veterans Administration hospital was Dr. Joseph H. Ward. In 1922, Dr. Ward was named superintendent of the Tuskegee (Alabama) Veterans Hospital. During his twelve years as head of the Tuskegee facility, he made an enviable record. Dr. Ward died on December 12, 1956, in Indianapolis, Indiana, at the age of eighty-six.

The first person to develop the blood bank was Dr. Charles Drew, a Negro. Drew introduced the use of plasma on the battlefield, organized the world's first mass blood bank project— Blood for Britain—and established the American Red Cross Blood Bank, of which he was the first director. Today, due to Dr. Drew's introduction of blood plasma, countless lives have been saved.

Born in Washington, D.C., on June 3, 1904, Drew graduated from Amherst College in Massachusetts, where he received the Messman Trophy for having brought the most honor to the school during his four years there. He was not only an outstanding scholar but also the captain of the track team and star halfback on the football team. After receiving his medical degree in 1933 from McGill University in Montreal, Canada, Drew returned to Washington to teach pathology at Howard University. In 1940, while taking his D.Sc. degree at Columbia University, he wrote a dissertation on "banked blood," and soon became such an expert in this field that the British government called upon his services to set up the first blood bank in England.

During World War II, Dr. Drew was appointed director of the American Red Cross blood donor project. In response to an armed forces dictum that only Caucasian blood would be acceptable, Dr. Drew called a press conference and spoke "not as a Negro but as a scientist." He told reporters, "I will not give you an opinion. I will give you scientific facts. The blood of individual human beings may differ by blood groupings, but there is absolutely no scientific basis to indicate any difference according to race."

After resigning from his post as Red Cross director of blood banks, Drew rejoined the Howard faculty and gained new prominence as head of the university's department of surgery, and as chief surgeon, chief of staff, and medical director of Freedman's Hospital, associated with Howard University.

In 1950, Dr. Drew was on his way to a medical meeting at Tuskegee Institute in Alabama, when his car overturned. Five white hospitals refused to admit him. The result was that he bled to death.

The first medical clinical laboratory at Northwestern University Medical School was organized by Dr. Theodore K. Lawless, the noted Negro dermatologist. He was an instructor in the school's Dermatology Department between 1924 and 1940, and was recipient of an Elizabeth J. Ward Fellowship from Northwestern Medical School, 1930–40.

Dr. Lawless was born in Thibodeaux, Louisiana, in 1892. He was educated at Talledega College in Alabama, the University of Kansas, Columbia University, and Harvard. He received his M.D. degree from Northwestern University Medical School in 1919, and his M.S. in Medicine from Northwestern in 1920. He received additional postgraduate training at the universities of Paris, Freiburg, and Vienna. Dr. Lawless has made signal contributions in the scientific treatment of syphilis and leprosy. For many years he has been senior attending physician at Provident Hospital.

Dr. Lawless was the insipration for the establishment of the Lawless Memorial Chapel, Dillard University, New Orleans, Louisiana; the Lawless Department of Dermatology in Beilison Hospital, Tel-Aviv, Israel; the Dr. T. K. Lawless Student Summer Program at the Weizmann Institute of Science, Rehovoth, Israel; the Lawless Clinical and Research Laboratory in Dermatology of the Hebrew Medical School, Jerusalem; and the chemical laboratory and lecture auditorium at Roosevelt University in Chicago.

On October 31, 1969, the famed dermatologist was honored at the annual Founder's Day ceremonies of Loyola University. He was cited for his dedication and acclaimed service to the medical specialty of dermatology.

◆

The first Negro woman to graduate from Harvard University Medical School was Dr. Mildred Fay Jefferson. She graduated in June, 1951. Dr. Jefferson was born in Texas, and received her A.B. degree from Texas College and her M.S. degree from Tufts University in Massachusetts.

◆

The first Negro woman to graduate from a formerly all-white Southern medical school was Dr. Edith Irby Jones, who graduated from the University of Arkansas School of Medicine in 1952. Dr. Jones set another "first" by becoming the first Negro to intern at the university hospital there. This woman, who made educational history in the South, was born in Conway, Arkansas, and was graduated with a B.S. degree from Knoxville (Tennessee) College.

She completed her graduate study at Northwestern University in Evanston, Illinois.

◆

The first Negro physician in the nation to be elected to the House of Delegates, the policymaking body of the American Medical Association, was Dr. Peter Marshall Murray. In 1954, he was the first black president of the New York County Medical Society, and in 1958 he became the first of his race to serve on the City Board of Hospitals, the decision-making body of the Department of Hospitals in New York City. A diplomate of the American Board of Obstetrics and Gynecology, he directed that department at Harlem Hospital until 1952. In 1969, the New York Academy of Medicine, of which he was a member, presented a plaque to Murray in appreciation of his services.

Born in Houma, Louisiana, Dr. Murray had his roots in New Orleans, where his parents had moved during his boyhood years. It was his mother's work at the old New Orleans Hospital and Dispensary for Women and Children, later to become Sara Mayo Hospital, which directed his path into medicine.

Dr. Murray earned his bachelor's degree in 1910 at New Orleans University, a forerunner of Dillard University, and received his medical education in 1914 at Howard University's Medical School. He interned at Freedmen's Hospital in Washington and remained on its staff as assistant clinical professor of surgery and assistant surgeon-in-chief until 1920. From Washington he went to New York to spend the balance of his forty-two years in medicine, a physician of note and a worker at lowering the bars of racial discrimination. Dr. Murray died in December, 1969, at the age of eighty-one.

◆

The first Negro president of the International Association of Dental Research was Dr. Clifton O. Dummett of Los Angeles, California. The Guiana-born professor, who is chairman of the University of Southern California's community dentistry department, was voted president by the two thousand-member group in July, 1969. Dr. Dummett received his degree in periodontics from Northwestern University. He served as dean of Meharry Medical College's School of Dentistry; this appointment, at the age of twenty-eight, made him the youngest man ever to head a dental

school in the U.S. Before he became a professor at USC, Dummett
served as chief of dental service in the Veterans Administration at
Tuskegee, Alabama.

Merchant Ships

The first merchant ship of the United States commanded by a
Negro captain was the *Booker T. Washington,* a Liberty ship
launched by the California Shipbuilding Corporation at Wilmington, Delaware, on September 29, 1942. It was commanded by
Captain Hugh Mulzac, the first Negro to hold an unlimited
mariner's license. It arrived at her first port, London, England, on
February 12, 1943.

Under Mulzac's command the vessel transported eighteen
thousand troops to the Mediterranean, France, England, and the
Pacific, and made more than twenty-two round trips.

Earlier, in 1939, Captain Mulzac had been cited by the New
York chapter of the Association for the Study of Negro Life and
History "for bringing honor and hope to black seamen." Captain
Mulzac died at his home in East Meadow, Long Island, at the age
of eighty-four in January, 1971.

Methodist Church

The first converted Negro Methodist was baptized in England
by John Wesley, who wrote in his diary on November 29, 1758: "I
rode to Wandsworth, and baptized two Negroes belonging to Mr.
Gilbert, a gentleman lately from Antigua. One of these was deeply
convinced of sin; the other is rejoicing in God, her savior, and is
the first African Christian I have known. But shall not God, in his
own time, have these heathen also for his inheritance?"

◆

The first Methodist congregation in the United States had a
Negro as one of its members. Betty, a Negro servant girl, was one
of the five members who met in the private house of Philip
Embury, in New York, in 1766. This group later became the John
Street Methodist Church—the oldest Methodist Church in the
country.

◆

The first separate Negro Methodist Church was organized at Wilmington, Delaware, in 1813. It was known as the Union American Methodist Episcopal Church.

◆

The first two Negro bishops in the Methodist Episcopal Church were Robert Elijah Jones and Matthew W. Clair. They were elected by the General Conference of the church in 1920. Of this event, Bishop Thirkield, Bishop Jones' predecessor in the region to which Bishop Jones was assigned said: "The election of two colored bishops by the great Methodist Episcopal Church is the most significant event in the religious history of the Negro since emancipation. Their election by a body of 800 delegates from the whole world, not grudgingly, but with contagious enthusiasm and the vision of its significance as related to the whole world, is an event of far-reaching importance. It forever gives assurance that ours is not a white man's church but a church as broad as humanity and all-inclusive as the redemptive blood of Jesus Christ."

Robert Elijah Jones was born in North Carolina in 1872, and educated at Bennett and Gammon colleges. Prior to his elevation to the bishopric, he served as editor of the *South Western Christian Advocate,* one of the best Negro journals in the country. Bishop Jones was given charge of the Negro Methodist churches of Louisiana and adjacent parts of the South, taking the diocese presided over formerly by Bishop Thirkield.

Matthew W. Clair was born in West Virginia in 1865, and educated at Morgan College. For seventeen years he was pastor of Ashbury Church in Washington, where he erected a new edifice. At the time of his election, he was serving as district superintendent. Bishop Clair was assigned to Liberia for a period of four years.

◆

The first two Negro bishops named to head predominantly white areas in the Methodist Church were James S. Thomas and Prince Taylor, Jr. In Cleveland, delegates to the Midwest meeting in 1964 voted unanimously to incorporate Negro churches and pastors, and assigned Bishop James S. Thomas, forty-five years old, to head the Iowa area. A native of South Carolina, Bishop

Thomas presides over 300,000 Methodists (all but 500 of them white) from a headquarters in Des Moines. A few days previous to Thomas' assignment, in the Northeast, white Methodists also accepted Negro churches in their jurisdiction and appointed Bishop Prince Taylor, Jr., of Baltimore to head the newly created New Jersey district. He presides over more than 600 churches with 200,000 members, only about five percent of them Negro.

See also Sunday Schools.

Money

America's first Negro millionaire was William Alexander Leidesdorff. He was born in 1810, at St. Croix in the Virgin Islands. He made his fortune as a cotton merchant in New Orleans after—legend has it—an unhappy love affair.

Arriving in San Francisco in 1841, Leidesdorff immediately set about acquiring real estate. In the short period of seven years, he became a successful merchant, diplomat, city councilman, and city treasurer. Also he was chairman of the school board that opened the state's first public school in April, 1848.

In May, 1848, Leidesdorff died of typhus. He was buried beneath the floor of the Mission Dolores in California. A wide-ranging legal battle developed over his estate, which eventually was bought by Army Captain Joseph Folsom for $75,000. Deeds later placed the value of Leidesdorff's property at $1.5 million.

◆

The first Negro whose signature appeared on U.S. currency was Blanche K. Bruce, a Mississippi politician who rose from state senator to U.S. senator. He was named registrar of the Treasury by President James Garfield in 1881, and served a five-year period. He was then appointed to serve another term in 1898.

◆

The first coin bearing the portrait of a Negro was the fifty-cent silver commemorative honoring Booker T. Washington. On August 7, 1946, President Harry Truman authorized the coinage of fifty-cent pieces "to commemorate the life and perpetuate the ideals and teachings of Booker T. Washington." The first coin was presented to President Truman on December 17, 1946. The obverse showed the head of Washington and the reverse a stylized Hall of Fame, under which were the words "From Slave Cabin to Hall of Fame." Centered under this wording was a slave cabin, to the left of which was "In God We Trust," and to the right, "Franklin County, Virginia." Around the rim was "Booker T. Washington Birthplace Memorial."

Not only was this coin the first issued by the United States mint bearing the likeness of a Negro, but it was also the first designed by a member of the Negro race. The designer was Isaac Hathaway, a member of the faculty at Tuskegee Institute. The Philadelphia and San Francisco coins were sold for a dollar each; the Denver coins, for one dollar and a half.

Monuments

The first national monument dedicated to a Negro was the George Washington Carver National Monument, authorized on July 14, 1943, officially established on June 14, 1951, and dedicated on July 14, 1955, near Diamond in southwest Missouri. It is administered by the National Park Service of the Department of the Interior. In addition to being the first national monument to an American Negro, it was also the first such tribute to an American scientist for services to agriculture.

◆

The first memorial to a black American on public land in the nation's capital will be a statue of Mary McLeod Bethune, a Methodist woman who "epitomized the black man's quest for dignity and justice." Ground was broken for the memorial on June 19, 1971, in Lincoln Square, a mile east of the United Methodist Building on Capitol Hill.

Mrs. Bethune, born in 1874 of slave parentage, founded Bethune Cookman College at Daytona Beach, Florida, and served as advisor to four U.S. presidents. She also founded in 1935 the National Council of Negro Women, which united black women to deal with problems of the black community. The Council spearheaded the drive for the memorial to Mrs. Bethune.

The Women's Division of the Methodist Church authorized a special appeal for $100,000 for the memorial project, from members of the Women's Society and Guild, to honor Mrs. Bethune's "contribution to church and society."

Music

Negro spirituals are often hailed by historians as the first American music. In his famous essay, "Of the Sorrow Songs," W. E. B. Du Bois called the spirituals the "music of an unhappy people, of the children of disappointment; they tell of death and suffering and unvoiced longing toward a truer world, of misty wanderings and hidden ways." The chief characteristic of the spirituals is melody. "Steal Away to Jesus," "Swing Low, Sweet Chariot," "Nobody Knows de Trouble I See," "Go Down, Moses," "I Couldn't Hear Nobody Pray," "Deep River," "O Freedom Over Me," and many others of these songs possess a beauty that is sublime.

The original Jubilee Singers from Fisk University introduced these songs to the musical world in 1871, through singing tours arranged to raise money for their new school.

Negro spirituals are traceable to Africa. H. E. Krehbiel, the nineteenth-century pioneer authority on the Afro-American folksongs, analyzed 527 Negro spirituals and found their identical prototypes in African music, concluding that the essential "intervallic rhythmical and structural elements" came from the ancestral homelands. These vestiges of African music rose to a higher harmonic development when there was fused into them the spirit of Christianity as the Negro slaves knew it. At this moment in their history there was at hand the precise religion for the adverse conditions into which they found themselves thrust. This religion imparted the hope that in the next world there would be a reversal of conditions. All men—slave and free, black and white, rich and poor, high and low—would be equal. The result was a body of song voicing all the cardinal virtues of Christianity—forgiveness, tolerance, patience, forebearance, love, faith, and hope—through a necessarily modified musical form brought from Africa. The Negro took complete refuge in Christianity, and the spirituals were literally forged out of sorrow in the heat of religious fervor. They brought hope and comfort to a burdened people.

Harry T. Burleigh, one of the greatest songwriters of the first three decades of the twentieth century, was one of the first to harmonize spirituals in such a way as to retain their natural simplicity and at the same time to enhance those qualities which made them universally loved. For around a half century, he was baritone soloist at St. George Protestant Episcopal Church in New York City; for twenty-five years he also sang in the choir at Temple Emanu-El in New York. His melodious singing brought about greater harmony among the races and contributed to a spirit of mutual goodwill. When Burleigh was on a concert tour of Europe, he sang for King Edward VII on two occasions.

◆

Negro slaves gave birth to the first calypso songs. A night after a full day's work in fierce tropical sunshine, the slaves gathered in groups outside their crude tapir huts and chanted songs to the beat of their drums. These were songs of good-humored banter and praise, which the African slaves called "calypsoes," derived from an African word meaning "brave."

◆

The first popularizer of Negro songs was Johann Christian Gotlieb Graupner, a Negro, who became known as the "Father of Negro, songs." On December 30, 1799, at the Federal Street Theatre in Boston, Massachusetts, he sang "The Gay Negro Boy" in the second act of *Oroonoko,* accompanying himself on the banjo. His excellent reception induced him to specialize in popularizing Negro songs.

◆

The first American Negro musician to win more than local recognition was Elizabeth Taylor Greenfield, the concert singer. She was born a slave in Natchez, Mississippi, in 1809, but at the age of one year was taken to Philadelphia by a Quaker woman and educated in freedom. Her fine voice earned for her the title, "The Black Swan." In the course of a European tour she sang before Queen Victoria at Buckingham Palace in 1854. She died in 1876.

◆

The first Negro pianist to win national fame was Thomas Bethune, better known as Blind Tom. Born blind in 1848, the twentieth child of a slave woman in Georgia, he was considered worthless and thrown into the bargain when his mother was sold to a Colonel Bethune. As an infant, Tom was enthralled by the piano playing of Bethune's daughters and early demonstrated a fantastic talent for complete recall and for reproducing on the piano whatever music he heard, besides contriving extraordinary improvisations. He was said by some to be the greatest untaught musical genius of all time. Although illiterate as well as blind, he had perfect pitch, and played some five thousand classical selections from memory. He could perform any piece perfectly after hearing it played once. He is reputed to have played in 1860 for President Buchanan. After the war, Bethune persuaded Tom's mother to designate him as guardian of the "idiotic Tom." This meant increasing exploitation. Touring the world, Tom earned $100,000 for his guardian in a single year. He died in 1905, at the age of fifty-nine.

◆

The first state whose official song was written by a Negro was Virginia. The song was "Carry Me Back to Old Virginny," and was written by James Bland.

Born in Flushing, New York, on October 22, 1854, Bland moved to Washington, D.C., at an early age. His father, Allan M. Bland, was one of the country's earliest Negro college graduates and the first Negro examiner in the U.S. Patent Office. Bland himself attended Howard University, studying music and beginning to create his own tunes. He wrote close to 700 songs altogether. Some of his more widely known are "Hand Me Down My Walking Cane," "Dem Golden Slippers," "In the Evening by the Moonlight," and "The Dandy Black Brigade." He was a performer as well as a composer. The banjo, invented by a slave, was at that time a four-string instrument; Bland added a fifth string and created a more versatile instrument. In 1881, he toured England and was such a success that he decided to stay. He became one of England's most famous entertainers, and gave a command performance for Queen Victoria and the Prince of Wales. After a spectacular career as a minstrel, he died penniless in 1911. In 1946, he was honored by the Lions Club of Virginia, and a monument was erected over his grave in Balacynwyd, Pennsylvania.

◆

The first Negro opera troupe was The Colored American Opera Company formed in Washington, D.C., in 1873. This troupe was composed of some of the most talented amateur musicians residing in that city.

The first performances were given in Lincoln Hall, Washington, on the evenings of February 3, and 4, 1873 consisting of Eichberg's opera, *The Doctor of Alcantara.* The company's next performances were at Agricultural Hall in Philadelphia, on February 21, 22, and 23. The troupe returned to Washington, where the two last performances of the series were given in Ford's Theatre.

◆

The first important book on the Negro in music, *Music and Some Highly Musical People,* was written by James M. Trotter in 1881. *The Literary World* of Boston, Massachusetts, speaking of this work, said:

> "Music and Some Highly Musical People"—We were disposed to give this book a generous reception before reading it, for its author's sake; and now, after reading, we give it a hearty commendation for its own. It is a well-conceived and well-constructed essay, in an entirely new direction, combining some really useful qualities in a truly clever way. Mr. Trotter is an African by race, now occupying, (we believe) a position in the Boston postoffice; and his aim in this work is to show what is being done by his people in the musical profession. Of its three parts, the first—an essay proper, critical and historical—and the third—a collection of musical compositions by different hands—are of the least value. The second, which is by far the larger portion of the volume, comprising biographical and critical sketches of a large number of "highly musical (colored) people," brings together a mass of curious, interesting and valuable information, which it would probably be impossible to duplicate in any one place elsewhere.

Trotter was born in Grand Gulf, Mississippi, in 1844, and spent his early days in Cincinnati, Ohio, until about twelve years of age. He moved to Hamilton, Ohio, where he attended school and studied music and developed a deep interest in musical art. He finally moved to Massachusetts. When the war broke out, Trotter enlisted in the army as a private in the Fifty-fourth Massachusetts and rose to the rank of lieutenant. After the war, the Republican party rewarded him by appointing him assistant superintendent of the registered letter department in the Boston post office, a position which he held for eighteen years. In 1887, he was appointed recorder of deeds by President Grover Cleveland. He died in 1912.

◆

Jazz was originated by black musicians in the Storyville section of New Orleans in the late 1800's. Its music was created out of African rhythms brought here by the Negroes. Charles "Buddy" Bolden, born in 1868, in the rough-and-ready uptown section of New Orleans, organized the first out-and-out jazz band around 1897. He was the first jazzman to earn the title "King" by popular acclaim. For seven years he was the undisputed champion. Then, at the age of twenty-nine, he ran amuck during a parade and was committed to the state hospital at Angola on June 5, 1907. He died twenty-four years later.

◆

The "blues" were first popularized by W. C. Handy, a Negro musician who was born in Florence, Alabama. He wrote his "Memphis Blues" in 1909, which was originally called "Mr. Crump," after the most famous of all Memphis politicians. Handy decided to make Memphis his headquarters and opened up the offices of the Pace and Handy Music Company, writers and sellers of songs. The company skyrocketed to success within a year, for among the many compositions Handy produced was the "St. Louis Blues," which was an instant success and won for him the title, "Father of the Blues." Although Handy wrote sixty other songs, his work was by no means limited to blues. He is the composer of "Aframerican Hymn," "Blue Destiny" (a symphonic piece), and over 150 other famous compositions, both sacred and secular.

In 1931, the city of Memphis, Tennessee, named a park after Handy. Sixteen years later a huge theater in Memphis was given his name. In Florence, Alabama, stands the W. C. Handy School. Handy died in 1958, but the melodies he contributed remain as a vital part of America's musical heritage.

◆

The first Negro to attain notable success as a singer of songs by composers of all nationalities and all epochs was Roland Hayes. Other Negro singers had previously attempted to do this, but he was the first to succeed in a notable way. He has been called "the greatest tenor ever born in America."

Hayes was born of former slave parents in Curryville, Georgia, on June 3, 1887. His career began in the Mount Zion Baptist Church in Curryville, Georgia, where he led the singing of spirituals. Some thirty years later he was singing in the palaces of Europe. In between came work in a Chattanooga window sash factory (where the sound of a friend's Caruso records opened new worlds), enrollment at Fisk University in Nashville, and, after a tour of Boston with the Fisk Jubilee Singers in 1911, the serious decision to settle there and secure competent training for his voice.

In 1917, he became the first Negro to give a recital in Boston's Symphony Hall. Three years later he traveled to London and gave a royal command performance, following this with other successes on the Continent. These enhanced his professional career enormously. Once financially successful, Hayes followed a policy of low-cost admissions so that the poor of all races could hear him.

In June, 1924, it was announced that Roland Hayes had been chosen as Spingarn Medalist for the year 1923. He could not at that time be present in person, so that the medal was actually handed to him on April 7, 1925, by Walter Damrosch, one of America's most eminent musicians, who on March 27 had celebrated his fortieth year as conductor of the New York Symphony Orchestra. After the medal had been presented to Hayes, he began to speak in an even calm tone:

> It is now nearly twenty years since I entered upon my artistic career. I did it because I had the conviction that my talent was the gift of an Infinite Mind and that it had been entrusted to me for a divine purpose, and that purpose was that the various racial groups that make up the human family should be served with the highest expression of that gift.
>
> Recognizing that the fact I have striven without thought of honor, save that honor which comes by achievement.
>
> By this, dear friends, you will understand what a tremendous surprise it was to me when I learned that the Spingarn Medal Award Committee of the National Association for the Advancement of Colored People had recognized my achievements to be worthy of this most significant honor. Indeed, it is a great honor, and yet not any part of that honor can I accept, except with the understanding that the honor which the award carries with it includes all of the colored people of these United States and the world so far as my talent has been recognized, because that which you recognize of merit in my work is that which you yourselves

have helped me to bring into a vivid, conscious existence, through me, a living instrument.

Hayes returned to Fisk in 1932 to receive an honorary doctorate in music. Ohio, Wesleyan, Boston, Howard, and Temple universities have also bestowed honorary degrees upon him.

On his seventy-fifth birthday, June 3, 1962, Hayes gave a program of lieder and spirituals at Carnegie Hall sponsored by the American Missionary Association College Centennials Fund, and received the first Amistad Award for contributing creatively to the improvement of human relations. Overwhelmed by the acclaim, Hayes confidently declared: "My commencement will be when I'm eighty."

The first series of recordings by a Negro jazz group were made by the Creole Jazz Band in 1923. Joseph (King) Oliver was the director. Oliver also helped Louis Armstrong become famous as a jazz artist.

The first jazzman to achieve recognition on the soprano saxophone was Sidney Bechet. Bechet was born in 1897, and died in 1959. He was also the first Negro to win acceptance in classical circles as a serious musician.

The first musician to adapt the jazz trombone to the demanding techniques called for by the advent of bop was a Negro born in 1924. J. J. Johnson—the unchallenged master of this instrument.

The first black man to receive an honorary Doctor of Music degree from the School of Music of Oberlin College was R. Nathaniel Dett.

The first symphony on a Negro folk theme was the *Symphony No. 1* (the Negro Folk Symphony) composed by the famous Negro conductor, William Levi Dawson. It was first presented on November 14, 1934, by the Philadelphia Orchestra under the direction of Leopold Stokowski at the Academy of Music in Philadelphia.

Born in Anniston, Alabama, in 1898, William Dawson ran away from home to attend Tuskegee Institute. At Tuskegee he took a job caring for the instruments of the Institute band; he learned to play most of them. After finishing Tuskegee in 1921, he attended Horner Institute of Fine Arts in Kansas City as an irregular student. Then, taking a leave of absence from a teaching post, he went to Chicago and entered both a municipal junior college and the American Conservatory of Music. While carrying on this double program, he made a living by playing at a dance hall, directing a Negro church choir, and playing the trombone as the only Negro member of the Chicago Civic Orchestra. Returning to Kansas City, he completed the course at Horner, graduating with honors. However, he was not permitted to sit on the platform with his white classmates when the governor of the state distributed the diplomas. Neither was he allowed to acknowledge the spirited applause that followed the Kansas City Symphony's performance of a composition for which he had been awarded a price in Chicago. Sitting beside him in the audience, speechless with amazement, was Roy Wilkins, then a young Kansas City journalist.

Among Dawson's compositions are "I Couldn't Hear Nobody Pray" and "Talk About a Child That Do Love Jesus, Here Is One." His most notable symphonic work is *Negro Folk Symphony No. 1*. For many years Dawson was director of music at Tuskegee Institute. With his compositions and arrangements he made the Tuskegee Institute Choir one of the nation's finest. Following his retirement from active direction of the choir in 1955, Dawson was sent to Spain by the U.S. State Department to train Spanish choral groups in the singing of Negro spirituals.

◆

The first Negro to conduct a major symphony orchestra in the United States was William Grant Still, who in 1936 directed the Los Angeles Philharmonic Orchestra in his own compositions in the Hollywood Bowl.

Still was born on May 11, 1895, in Woodville, Mississippi and educated in the public schools of Little Rock, Arkansas. He attended Wilberforce University and then studied at the Oberlin Conservatory of Music and the New England Conservatory. He studied privately with George W. Chadwick and Edgard Varèse, both of whom granted him scholarships. He learned to orchestrate by playing many instruments (among them the violin, cello, and oboe) in professional orchestras, and by orchestrating for W. C. Handy, Don Voorhees, Sophie Tucker, Paul Whiteman, Willard Robinson, and Artie Shaw. For several years he arranged and conducted the "Deep River Hour" over CBS and WOR radio stations.

Still is a member of ASCAP and the League of Composers, the recipient of extended Guggenheim and Rosenwald Fellowships, of the honorary degrees of Master of Music (from Wilberforce University, 1936), Doctor of Music (from Howard University, 1941), and from Oberlin College (1947), of the second Harmon award (1927), as well as a trophy of honor from Local 767 of the Musicians' Union AF of M, of which he is a member. He has won important commissions from the Columbia Broadcasting System, the New York World's Fair, 1939–40, Paul Whiteman, the League of Composers, and the Cleveland Orchestra.

On April 16, 1968, Still conducted some of his own works as guest conductor of the New Orleans Philharmonic Symphony in a concert sponsored by Dillard University at McAlister Auditorium on the Tulane University campus. This marked the first time that a Negro conducted the orchestra in New Orleans.

Still is known for many works. Among these are *Troubled Island,* an opera with a 1791 Haitian setting; *Highway No. 1, U.S.A.,* an opera first presented in Miami in 1963; *Lenox Avenue, La Guiblesse, Sahdji,* and *Miss Sally's Party,* all ballets; and *Afro-American Symphony,* perhaps his best-known composition for a large orchestra.

◆

The first Negro American to win international acclaim as a symphonic conductor was Dean Dixon.

Dixon was born in Harlem on January 10, 1915, to highly educated West Indian parents. He graduated from DeWitt Clinton High School in 1932. Exposed to classical music by his parents (as a small boy he was regularly taken to Carnegie Hall), Dixon formed his own amateur orchestra at the Harlem YMCA while he was still in high school. On the basis of a successful violin audition, he was admitted to the Juilliard Institute of Musical Art, where he received his B.S. in 1936. Three years later he acquired his master's degree from Columbia University.

The Dean Dixon Symphony Society, which he had formed in 1932, began to receive financial support from the Harlem community in 1937, and, in 1941, at the request of Eleanor Roosevelt, Dixon gave a concert at the Heckscher Theater. In the same year, Dixon became the first Negro and, at twenty-six, the youngest musician ever to conduct the one-hundred-year-old New York Philharmonic Orchestra. In 1948, he received the $1,000 Alice M. Ditson Award as the outstanding music conductor of the year.

Dixon left America in 1949, because he could not find a regular post as a symphonic conductor despite his admittedly great talents. In Europe he conducted leading orchestras in Austria, Germany, Belgium, Czechoslovakia, Denmark, Hungary, Spain, England, Finland, France, Holland, Italy, Monaco, Norway, Poland, Switzerland, and Yugoslavia. He also conducted in Israel, Mexico, Argentina, and Australia. Though an expatriate, Dixon is regarded as an ambassador of American music. He has introduced more than fifty contemporary American works to continental audiences. He still dreams of returning to the land of his birth, "leading my own symphony."

◆

The first Negro to sing a white role with a white cast in an opera company was Robert Todd Duncan, a baritone of Washington, D.C., who first appeared as Conio in *I Pagliacci* on September 28, 1945, and as Escamillo in *Carmen* on September 30, 1945, in the New York City Opera Company's presentation at the City Center of Music and Drama in New York City.

Todd Duncan was born into a well-to-do family in Danville, Kentucky, on February 12, 1903. He received his first lessons from his mother, who was a music teacher, but not until his student days at Butler University in Indianapolis did he become seriously interested in a musical career. He studied voice and theory at an Indianapolis conservatory, and after receiving a master's degree at Columbia University went to Howard University as a voice teacher. An appearance in a Negro production of *Cavalleria Rusticana* in New York in 1935 brought him to the attention of George Gershwin, who promptly engaged him for the male lead in his *Porgy and Bess.* Duncan was such a success that he repeated his performance in this role in the 1938 and 1942 revivals of the play. In 1940, he was a featured performer on Broadway in *Cabin in the Sky.* When the play closed he headed for Hollywood to appear in the movie *Syncopation.*

◆

The first Negro to sing at the Metropolitan Opera was Marian Anderson. In 1955, after years of successful concert work, she made her Metropolitan debut in Verdi's *The Masked Ball.*

Marian Anderson was born of poor parents on February 27, 1902, in Philadelphia. When she was twelve, her father died. To keep the home together, Mrs. Anderson went to work. Miss Anderson says that the happiest moment of her life came on the day that she was able to tell her mother to stop working. Shortly after her father's death, Marian was converted to her father's Union Baptist Church, largely because the late Reverend Wesley G. Parks was deeply interested in music, loved his choirs, and encouraged any outstanding singer in them. At thirteen, Marian was singing in the church's choir. At fifteen, she took her first formal music lesson. At sixteen, she gave her first important concert, at a Negro school in Atlanta. It was the congregation of the Union Baptist Church that gave Miss Anderson her start. Then a group of interested music lovers sponsored a concert for her at her church, and collected about $500 to pay for training her voice under the late Philadelphia singing teacher, Giuseppe Boghetti. Four lears later she appeared as soloist with the New York Philharmonic. After a short engagement with the Philadelphia Symphony Orchestra, she traveled to Europe on a scholarship granted by the National Association of Negro Musicians.

On Easter Sunday in 1939 Miss Anderson gave what is perhaps her most memorable concert. She sang on the steps of the Lincoln Memorial after having been barred from making an appearance at Constitution Hall by the Daughters of the American Revolution because of her race.

Her early audiences were all-Negro, but later she was heard primarily by white or unsegregated groups, and eventually she declined to sing at all before houses where segregation was enforced. This decision did not eliminate her concerts in the South, for she sang occasionally before mixed audiences in college, church, and town auditoriums. When her native city gave her the $10,000 Bok Award, annually given to the year's most distinguished Philadelphian, she established a scholarship that has enabled many young Negroes to secure musical training.

Miss Anderson has received a total of twenty-one honorary doctorate degrees. Says she, "If only a comparable amount of

knowledge would go with each of them." In 1958, President
Eisenhower named her to the U.S. Mission to the United Nations.
Admitted the great lady, "We are honored."

Appropriately, Miss Anderson gave her farewell performance
on Easter Sunday in 1965 at New York's Carnegie Hall. She then
retired with her husband to their farm in Danbury, Connecticut.

◆

For the first time in modern history the names of many of the
greats of Negro music were placed into the *Congressional Record*
by a congressman who lauded the tremendous contribution of the
Negro in the musical culture of this world.

On July 1, 1955, praising the U.S. Supreme Court desegregation ruling, Congressman Emanuel Celler (D., N.Y.) added the
following comments:

> Singers, bandleaders and composers who have enriched
> our popular music number among them many Negroes:
> Hazel Scott, Mary Lou Williams, Duke Ellington, Fats
> Waller, Louis Armstrong, Nat (King) Cole, Pearl Bailey and
> Count Basie, just to name a few. And not to be forgotten is
> W. C. Handy, who composed the perennial favorite "St.
> Louis Blues.
>
> In folklore and in spiritual, Negroes have left a mark on
> the musical history of our times. Harry T. Burleigh and R.
> Nathaniel Dett, through their arrangements of spirituals, did
> much to advance the popularity of the spiritual in concert
> repertoires. Various Negro choirs have gone on world tours
> and won high praise: notably, the Tuskegee, Hampton,
> Howard Fisk and Talladega University choirs and the Hall
> Johnson and Eva Jesse choirs. On the radio the Southenarires
> and the Wings Over Jordan Choir have maintained pro-
> longed popularity.

◆

The first Negro with his own television show (a musical
program) was Nat King Cole. The *Nat King Cole Show* on
NBC-TV ran from November, 1956, to December, 1957, and was
seen in some seventy-seven cities. Critics acclaimed its excellence,
and television rating services ranked it highly, but national sponsors
failed to materialize for fear of resentment by Southern whites.

Nathaniel Cole was born on March 17, 1919, in Montgomery,
Alabama. The family name was Coles, but Cole dropped the "s"
when he formed the King Cole Trio years later. Nat's mother, a

music teacher, gave him his first training, hoping he would become a classical pianist.

At the age of twelve, Nat was singing and playing the organ in the True Light Baptist Church, of which his father, the Reverend Edward James Coles, was pastor. As a student at Phillips High School he formed his own band.

In 1936, Cole joined the touring company of *Shuffle Along.* During the tour he was married to Nadine Robinson. Shortly afterward, the show folded in Long Beach, California. Cole then worked in small clubs there. The King Cole Trio was formed by accident in 1937 when the drummer in the quartet failed to appear for a scheduled performance. That same year, Cole made his singing debut when a customer requested "Sweet Lorraine," a number he later recorded with great success. Cole's first record was made in 1943. It was a song of his own composition with a title derived from one of his father's sermons, "Straighten Up and Fly Right." The song attained immediate popularity, and other records, compositions, and songs followed.

Cole's album of spirituals, *Every Time I Feel the Spirit,* a collection of the best-loved spirituals, including the title song. Among them are "I Want to Be Ready;" "Ain't Gonna Study War No More;" "Standing in the Need of Prayer;" and "Nobody Knows the Trouble I've Seen."

Cole experienced difficulties because of his race. When his family moved into Hancock Park, an exclusive area of Los Angeles which had previously been all-white, they at first met with considerable resentment from their neighbors.

In 1951, Cole filed suit in the Federal court against a hotel in Rock Island, Illinois, on the ground that he and the group traveling with him had been refused accommodations. Although the jury was deadlocked, the hotel immediately thereafter adopted a policy of integration, and Cole felt that he had won his point.

Cole died of cancer in 1965.

The first Negro from the world of jazz to receive the Spingarn Medal was Duke Ellington. He received the award in 1960. Ellington has been called "the most original music mind in America."

The "Duke" was born Edward Kennedy Ellington on April 29, 1899, in Washington, D.C. He earned the nickname "Duke" in school for his somewhat flamboyant attire. He evinced his creative talent early. At the age of seven, he was playing the piano, and at eighteen he composed his first piece, *The Soda Fountain Rag.* A talented painter, Ellington was offered a scholarship to the Pratt Institute of Fine Arts in New York City, but he decided instead to devote his life to music.

At twenty-four Ellington organized his own band, the Washingtonians; at twenty-eight he played at the Cotton Club, where his nationwide fame began. In the following years he toured through Europe as a concert artist. At the age of forty-four he performed the first of his many concerts at Carnegie Hall in New York City; and at forty-five he played for the first time at Chicago's Opera House and San Francisco's Philharmonic Hall. He celebrated his seventieth birthday as a guest of President Nixon at a "swinging" birthday party in the East Room of the White House. Ellington was the first living artist to sponsor a scholarship fund to the Juilliard School of Music.

Ellington has commented in regard to Negro music: "Remember that music speaks of emotions, ranging from grave to gay. Back in the forests and on the plains of Africa, the rhythm of nature surrounded the Negro in the dropping of water from a cliff and in the ominous measured beat of the tom-tom. Transplanted to the fields of the deep South, the Negroes of the slavery period were still moved by these influences and it is by these influences that their contribution to American music has been shaped. Because they remain so close to nature, they still express their emotions rhythmically."

In 1970, Duke Ellington was elected to membership in the National Institute of Arts and Letters, the nation's highest honor society of the arts.

He is the composer of the following songs: "Mood Indigo," "Solitude," "Sophisticated Lady," "Caravan," "I Let a Song Go Out of My Heart," "Do Nothing Till You Hear from Me," "Don't Get Around Much Anymore," "In a Sentimental Mood," "Black and White Fantasy," and "Creole Love Call."

He composed motion picture scores for *Anatomy of a Murder, Paris Blues,* and *Assault on a Queen.* He wrote extended orchestral jazz compositions and suites including *Reminiscing in Tempo,* 1935; *Black, Brown and Beige, A Tone Parallel to the History of the American Negro,* 1943; *New World Acoming,* 1945; *Liberian Suite,* 1948; *Harlem,* 1950. He conceived and wrote *A Concert of*

Sacred Music, which premiered at Grace Cathedral in San Francisco in 1965.

The first blacks to be hired by the Philadelphia Symphony Orchestra in the seventy years of its existence were Renard Edwards, 26, a viola player, and Booker T. Rowe, 29, a violinist. They received this recognition in 1970. Conductor Eugene Ormandy said: "They were chosen entirely because of their musical abilities. . . ."

See also Negro National Anthem.

Muslims (Black)

The first temple of Islam (Temple No. 1) for Black Muslims was founded in Detroit, Michigan, in 1931, by Elijah Muhammad, "Messenger of Allah."

Elijah Muhammad was born Elijah Poole in Sandersville, Georgia, on October 7, 1897. He completed the fourth grade at school before leaving home at the age of sixteen. In 1929, in Detroit, Poole met—according to his own statement—"Allah on earth" and, as a consequence of this meeting, proclaimed himself Allah's "messenger." Espousing a doctrine which has since been labeled "black supremacy" and "black separatism," Poole took the name Muhammad, dropping what he called his "slave-master name."

The National Association for the Advancement of Colored People (NAACP)

The first organization since abolitionism to provide a means for blacks and whites to cooperate in the work of securing and safeguarding the common citizenship rights of the Negro was the National Association for the Advancement of Colored People.

The immediate reason for forming this organization was the Springfield riots. In the summer of 1908, the country was shocked by the account of race riots at Springfield, Illinois. Here, in the home of Abraham Lincoln, a mob containing some of the town's "best citizens" raged for two days, killing and wounding scores of

Negroes and driving thousands from the city. Articles on the subject appeared in newspapers and magazines. Among them was one in the *Independent* of September 3, 1908, by William English Walling, a white southern writer with liberal views, entitled "Race War in the North." After describing the atrocities committed against the Negro people, Mr. Walling declared, "Either the spirit of the abolitionist, of Lincoln and of Lovejoy, must be revived and we must come to treat the Negro on a plane of absolute political and social equality or Vardaman and Tillman will soon have transferred the Race War to the North." He ended with these words, "Yet who realizes the seriousness of the situation and what large and powerful body of citizens is ready to come to their aid?"

The letter which eventually led to the founding of the NAACP was written to William E. Walling by Mary White Ovington, a wealthy young white woman from New York who had made a thorough study of racial problems and who had attended the 1906 meeting of the Niaraga group as a reporter for the *New York Evening Post*. In her letter she deplored the atrocities described by Walling in his article, and suggested that they explore what could be done to remedy the grievous state of race relations in the North and South.

Three people met in Walling's apartment in Manhattan in the first week of the new year, 1909, to discuss this grave situation. These three were William English Walling, Mary White Ovington and Henry Moskovitz, a Jewish social worker. All were concerned with democracy and the Negro. They decided to issue a call for a conference signed by a number of prominent Americans, to discuss racial grievances. This call was released on February 12, 1909, the one-hundredth anniversary of Abraham Lincoln's birth. Written by Oswald Garrison of the *New York Post*, the call read in part:

> The Celebration of the Centennial of the birth of Abraham Lincoln, widespread and grateful as it may be, will fail to justify itself if it takes no note of and makes no recognition of the colored men and women for whom the Great Emancipator labored to assure freedom. . . . If Mr. Lincoln could revisit this country in the flesh, he would be disheartened and discouraged. He would learn that on January 1, 1909, Georgia had rounded out a new confederacy by disfranchising the Negro, after the manner of all the other Southern States. He would learn that the Supreme Court of the United States, supposedly a bulwark of American liberties, had refused every opportunity to pass squarely

upon this disfranchisement of millions. . . . He would learn that the Supreme Court . . . had laid down the principle that if an individual State chooses, it may "Make it a crime for white and colored persons to frequent the same market place at the same time, or appear in an assemblage of citizens convened to consider questions of a public or political nature in which all citizens, without regard to race, are equally interested."

In many States Lincoln would see the black men and women, for whose freedom a hundred thousand soldiers gave their lives, set apart in trains, in which they pay first-class fares for third-class service, and segregated in railway stations and in places of entertainment; he would observe that State after State declines to do its elementary duty in preparing the Negro through education for the best exercise of citizenship. Added to this, the spread of lawless attacks upon the Negro, North, South, and West—even in the Springfield made famous by Lincoln . . . could but shock the author of the sentiment that "government of the people, by the people, for the people, should not perish from the earth."

Silence under these conditions means tacit approval. . . . Hence we call upon all the believers in democracy to join in a National Conference for the discussion of present evils, the voicing of protests, and the renewal of the struggle for civil and political liberty.

This document was signed by sixty Americans of distinction, including six Negroes: the Reverend William Henry Brooks; Alexander Walters, bishop of the African Methodist Episcopal Zion Church; Ida B. Wells Barnett; Mary Church Terrell; Dr. W. E. B. Du Bois; and Francis Grimke.

The conference that resulted from this call began on May 30, 1909, at the Henry Street Settlement in New York, and ended on June 1, with a mass meeting at Cooper Union. From these sessions there emerged an organization called the National Negro Committee.

At the second annual meeting of the National Negro Committee in May, 1910, a new name was chosen, the National Association for the Advancement of Colored People. As such the organization was incorporated under the laws of the state of New York and its officially recorded purposes were:

To promote equality of rights and eradicate caste or race prejudice among the citizens of the United States; to advance the interest of colored citizens; to secure for them impartial suffrage; and to increase their opportunities for securing justice in the courts, education for their children, employment according to their ability, and complete equality before the law.

◆

The first branch of the NAACP was established in Chicago, Illinois, three months after the organization was established. Within two years nine other branches had been formed. Each year, until the outbreak of World War I, the number of branches doubled.

◆

The first Negro officer of the NAACP was W. E. B. Du Bois who, in 1910, became its first director of publicity and research. In November of that same year, *The Crisis* was established, with Du Bois as its editor. This was the official organ of the NAACP. *The Crisis* took its name from "The Present Crisis," a poem by the abolitionist James Russell Lowell.

◆

The first Spingarn Award was given to Dr. Ernest E. Just for his outstanding achievements in biology. The award, instituted in 1914 by J. E. Spingarn, Chairman of the Board of Directors of the NAACP, is a gold medal given annually by this organization for the "highest or noblest achievement by an American Negro." The medal is intended to publicize and reward the distinguished accomplishments of Negroes in all fields of endeavor and to serve as an inspiration to Negro youth. This first award was presented to Dr. Just on February 12, 1915, at Ethical Culture Hall in New York City.

◆

The first major legal victory of the NAACP came in 1915, when the U.S. Supreme Court declared null and void the "Grandfather Clause" in the state constitutions of Oklahoma and Maryland, by which Negroes were barred from voting unless they could prove that their grandfathers had voted.

◆

The first Field Secretary of the NAACP was James Weldon Johnson, the writer, who accepted this newly created position in 1916, beginning what was to be his major work for the next fifteen years.

◆

The first public demonstration intended to arouse the conscience of the nation against the mounting number of lynchings and riots was the silent protest parade in New York sponsored by the NAACP in 1917. On a hot summer Saturday, ten thousand people marched down Fifth Avenue. Silent except for the sound of muffled drums, the parade was led by school children dressed in white. They carried signs reading: "Thou Shalt Not Kill," "Give Me a Chance to Live," and "Mother, Do Lynchers Go to Heaven?" Women in white followed the children. Men in mourning black brought up the rear. The demonstration attracted a huge crowd of spectators.

◆

The first Negro to be appointed to the position of Executive Secretary of the NAACP was James Weldon Johnson. He was appointed by the board of directors to succeed John Shillady in 1920.

◆

The first meeting of the National Association for the Advancement of Colored People to be held in the South was the annual conference of 1920, which met in Atlanta, Georgia, in May.

Negro

The term *Negro* is derived from the Spanish and Portuguese word "negro," meaning black. It is presumed to have been used first by explorers who sailed along the African coast for Prince Henry the Navigator of Portugal in the fifteenth century.

◆

The first recorded use of the word "Negro" in print is in Edein's *Decades* (1555): " They are not accustomed to eate such meates as doo the Ethiopians or Negroes."

The word "Negro" appears only once in the plays of Shakespeare. This is in the *Merchant of Venice* (written in 1595), Act III, Scene 5, line 42; yet its synonym "Moor" occurs some sixty times in Shakespeare's plays, mostly in *Othello,* but also in *Hamlet,* the *Merchant of Venice,* and *Titus Andronicus.*

◆

The first use of the word "Negro" in America, according to Lewis H. Michaux, owner of a book store called the House of Good Sense and Proper Propaganda, occurred in 1619, when a Dutch ship landed at the Jamestown Colony in Virginia with a cargo of twenty Africans who were brought here as indentured servants.

Negro National Anthem

The Negro National Anthem—"Lift Every Voice and Sing" was written by James Weldon Johnson, in Jacksonville, Florida, in 1900, to music composed by his brother H. Rosemond Johnson. The lyrics read:

> Lift every voice and sing.
> Till earth and heaven ring,
> Ring with the harmonies of Liberty;
> Let our rejoicing rise
> High as the listening skies,
> Let it resound loud as the rolling sea.
> Sing a song full of the faith that the dark past has taught us,
> Sing a song full of the hope that the present has brought us,
> Facing the rising sun of our new day begun
> Let us march on till victory is won.
>
> Stony the road we trod,
> Bitter the chastening rod,
> Felt in the days when hope unborn had died;
> Yet with a steady beat,
> Have not our weary feet
> Come to the place for which our fathers sighed?
> We have come over a way that with tears have been
>   watered,
> We have come, treading our path through the blood of the
>   slaughtered,
> Out from the gloomy past,
> Till now we stand at last
> Where the white gleam of our bright star is cast.
>
> God of our weary years,
> God of our silent tears,
> Thou who has brought us thus far on the way;
> Thou who has by Thy might
> Led us into the light,
> Keep us forever in the path, we pray.
> Lest our feet stray from the places, Our God, where we met
>   Thee,

Lest, our hearts drunk with the wine of the world, we
    forget Thee;
Shadowed beneath Thy hand,
May we forever stand.
True to our GOD,
True to our native land.

The song was written to be sung by a chorus of children from the
various schools of the city in honor of the anniversary of Abraham
Lincoln's birth. Neither the author nor the publisher anticipated
the fame it would eventually attain. The anthem spread throughout the South and then to the North as well, and has often been
sung by church choirs throughout the country.

Newspapers

The first newspaper edited by Negroes for Negroes was
Freedom's Journal, a four-page weekly published in New York City
from March 16, 1827, to March 28, 1829. Its editors were John
Brown Russwurm and Samuel E. Cornish. The tone of this newspaper was similar to Negro journalism today:

> The civil rights of a people being of the greatest value, it
> shall ever be our duty to vindicate our brethren, when
> oppressed; and to lay the case before the public with a view
> to arrest the progress of prejudice, and to shield ourselves
> against its consequent evils. We shall also urge upon our
> brethren (who are qualified by the laws of the different
> states) the expediency of using their elective franchise; and
> of making an independent use of the same. We wish them
> not to become the tools of party.

◆

The first Negro war correspondent in United States history was
T. Morris Chester, of New Orleans, who in 1863 joined the
Philadelphia Press and remained with it until the end of the Civil
War. It is said that his letter on the capture of Richmond by
General Grant was received twenty-four hours in advance of that
of any other correspondent.

◆

The first Negro daily in the United States was *La Tribune,*
which was first published in 1864 in New Orleans, Louisiana. Its
owner was Dr. L. C. Roudanez, a very active participant in early

Reconstruction politics, and its editor was Paul Trevigne, a school-teacher and writer for a daily white newspaper. *La Tribune* was published in French and English, as was customary for publications in that area at that time. Publication of *La Tribune* was suspended in 1868 owing to financial difficulties, and was resumed in 1869 for a brief period. It was a militant newspaper and was a strong champion for civil rights and universal suffrage.

◆

The first major city newspaper organized by Negroes for Negroes was the *Chicago Defender,* which was founded by Robert Abbot in 1905. The first issue was published on May 5.

◆

The first Negro foreign war correspondent in U.S. history was Joel A. Rogers, who was sent to Addis Ababa, Ethiopia, to report the Italo-Ethiopian War for the Pittsburgh *Courier,* in October, 1935. He returned on April 21, 1936.

Born in Jamaica, West Indies, in 1880, Rogers came to the United States in 1906, and became an American citizen in 1917. For more than fifty years he was one of the foremost Negro historians in the United States.

Rogers was the author of numerous newspaper and magazine articles and wrote an illustrated feature ("Your History") for the *Courier.* His books included *Superman to Man* (1917), *As Nature Leads* (1919), *World's Greatest Men of African Descent* (1935), *Sex and Race* (1940–1944), and *World's Great Men of Color* (1947).

He continued to work on a number of manuscripts until his death in New York City in January, 1966.

◆

The first Negro news correspondent accredited to the White House was Harry McAlpin, representing the Atlanta, Georgia, *Daily World* and the press service of the Negro Newspaper Publishers Association. He attended his first White House press conference on February 8, 1944.

◆

The first Negro news correspondent admitted to the House of Representatives and Senate press gallery was Percival L. Prattis, representative of *Our World,* New York City. He was accredited on February 3, 1947.

◆

The first black man to win the prestigious Pulitzer Prize for news feature photography since its inception in 1917 was Moneta Sleet, Jr., *Jet-Ebony* staff photographer. Sleet, who joined the Johnson Publishing Company in 1955, won the award with its $1,000 prize for his poignant photograph of Mrs. Coretta Scott King and her daughter, Bernice, at the funeral of her husband, the Reverend Dr. Martin Luther King, Jr., in Atlanta on April 9, 1968.

◆

The first Negro to be named city editor of the *Portland Oregonian* was William Hillard, who was named to this position in April, 1971, at the age of 43. His promotion stamps him as perhaps the highest ranking black newsman on an integrated major daily newspaper in the United States.

After obtaining his degree in journalism from Oregon's Pacific University, Hillard was hired as a copyboy on the *Oregonian* in 1952. After a brief stint in his position, he moved to sports writing. From sports he became a general assignment reporter, then church editor, and in 1962 became an assistant city editor.

In his new position, Hillard is responsible for all city news and the entire newsroom operation. He is in charge of nearly fifty reporters, columnists, and photographers. The *Oregonian* has a daily circulation of 250,000 and its Sunday circulation of more than 400,000 makes it the largest Sunday edition in the Northwest.

◆

The first black Religion Editor of the *Kansas City* (Kansas) *Star* was Helen T. Gott. She is the first and only black to hold such a post on this predominantly white Kansas City daily newspaper. Miss Gott, holder of a B.A. degree from Syracuse (N.Y.) University and a master's degree from Columbia University, began her duties June 1, 1971.

Niagara Movement

The first Negro protest organization in the twentieth century was the Niagara Movement. The group held its first meeting in Canada in June, 1905, because hotels on the New York State side of the falls did not admit Negroes. "We refuse to allow the impression to remain that the Negro American assents to inferiority, is submissive under oppression and apologetic before insults," said the Niagara platform, which W. E. B. Du Bois largely wrote.

The Niagara Movement represented a formal renunciation of the policy of accommodation which had been the keynote of Booker T. Washington's program for Negro advancement since his famed Atlanta Compromise address of 1895. The leaders of this new group called not for accommodation, but for immediate implementation of their civil rights. In the words of Du Bois:

> We want full manhood suffrage and we want it now. . . .
> We want the Constitution of the country enforced. . . .
> We want our children educated. . . . We are men! We will be treated as men. And we shall win.

The leaders of the Niagara Movement appended certain duties to its list of demands:

> The duty to vote.
> The duty to respect the rights of others.
> The duty to work.
> The duty to obey the laws.
> The duty to be clean and orderly.
> The duty to send our children to school.
> The duty to respect ourselves, even as we respect others.

In 1909, the Niagara Movement was absorbed into the framework of the National Association for the Advancement of Colored People, an organization founded on many of the same principles and whose foundations it helped to lay.

Nobel Peace Prize

The first American Negro to win the Nobel Prize was Ralph J. Bunche, whose mediations in 1949 between Israel and its Arab neighbors resulted in an armistice. The dispute had threatened to engulf the entire Middle East in armed conflict. On December 10, 1950, at Oslo, Norway, he received the Nobel Medal and diploma and a cash award equivalent to $31,674.80.

Bunche did his undergraduate work at the University of

California at Los Angeles. He earned his master's and Ph.D. degrees in political science from Harvard and did postdoctoral work at Northwestern University, the London School of Economics and the University of Cape Town in the Union of South Africa.

Before World War II broke out, Bunche did field work with the Swedish sociologist, Gunnar Myrdal, author of the widely acclaimed *An American Dilemma*. During the war itself, Bunche served initially as Senior Social Analyst for the Office of the Co-ordinator of Information in African and Far Eastern Affairs, anl was then reassigned to the African section of the Office of Strategic Services. In 1942, he helped draw up the territories and trusteeships section of the State Department ultimately earmarked for inclusion in the United Nations.

In 1955, Bunche was appointed U.N. Undersecretary for Special Political Affairs, a position requiring his services as principal adviser to the Secretary General of the United Nations. He has played a key role in the United Nations peace-keeping missions not only in the Middle East but in Cyprus, Yemen, the Congo, and other troubled spots.

In the summer of 1969, UCLA gave the name Ralph Bunche Hall to the tallest of seventy structures on its Westwood, California, campus when it renamed the eleven-story social science building in honor of its most distinguished black alumnus. When the campus officials dedicated the building in his name, Dr. Bunche commented: "One does not anticipate or even dream of an occasion of this kind. It is, therefore, something even beyond the fulfillment of a dream, and I know neither how to describe nor how to cope with it."

Nursing

The first black army nurse in U.S. history was Susie King Taylor who served with the First Regiment of the South Carolina Volunteers, the first black unit to fight in the Civil War.

Susie was born a slave on a plantation several miles from Savannah, Georgia, in 1848. She learned to read and write during her years in slavery, and taught these basic skills to many soldiers in the company. When the military hospital needed additional competent women to nurse the increasing number of wounded

Union troops, Susie quickly volunteered her services at Beaufort, South Carolina, in 1863.

Susie King was not a nurse in the technical sense. Yet months later, as her reputation spread, she was presented to Clara Barton (who later founded the Red Cross) as "one of the finest nurses we have in our regiment." Clara Barton shook Susie's hand and said, "I'm glad you are doing such a job. Some day I want you to become the first black nurse in this country."

Clara Barton, in the months ahead, took a personal interest in the eager young girl. "She was always very cordial." Susie wrote, "and I honored her for her devotion and care of the men."

When the war terminated, Susie went to Boston and worked as a maid.

One writer has observed in regard to Susie King:

> The story of Susie King Taylor . . . is just one more of the many sagas of black history in America which should have been revealed several generations ago. Susie Taylor's life is not only a great chapter in the black nursing profession, but it represents a vital part of the black man's role in America's military history, particularly the famous slave regiment led by Thomas Wentworth Higginson in the Civil War. . . .
>
> Susie had . . . an opportunity and proved her worth, not only as an individual performer in healing the sick and binding the wounds of the injured, but in training other black girls to do likewise.

Susie King Taylor died on October 6, 1912, in Boston.

◆

The first Negro graduate nurse in the United States was Mary E. Mahoney, who graduated from the New England Hospital for Women and Children in Roxbury, Massachusetts, in 1879. Born in Boston in 1845, Mary went to the hospital as a maid; later she was accepted as a student, and received her diploma. She won highest praise for her fight against color prejudice, her expert and tender care of the sick, and her encouragement of young people to go into nursing.

In her honor the Mary Mahoney Medal was founded by the American Nurses' Association and given biennially to the person making the most progress toward opening full opportunities in nursing for all, regardless of race, creed, color, or national origin.

Mary Mahoney passed away in 1925.

◆

The first training school for Negro nurses was the Spelman Seminary, in Atlanta, Georgia, founded in 1881 by Sophia Booker Packard and Harriet E. Giles of Boston, Massachusetts, as the Atlanta Baptist Female Seminary. In 1884 the name was changed to the Spelman Seminary and in 1924 to Spelman College, the name by which the institution is now known. A nurse's training department was established in 1886 in a two-room frame building set apart from an infirmary and known as the Everts Ward. The first nurse received her certificate in 1888.

◆

The first Negro to receive a certificate of registration as a trained nurse issued by authority of the State Board of Nurse Examiners of Tennessee was Minnie D. Woodward, a graduate of the nurse-training department of Meharry Medical College. The certificate was obtained in 1913, through the efforts of the Nashville Negro Board of Trade. Even after the board had won its case, objections arose from the white nurses in the state.

Olympics

The first time that a Negro ever won an Olympic medal was during the Olympic Games in 1932, in Los Angeles; at these games two Negroes won medals. Thomas Edward Tolan won two gold medals in track and field, one for the 100-meter run and the other for the 200-meter run. His teammate, Ralph Metcalfe, also won two medals, a silver one for the 100-meter run and a bronze one for the 200-meter run.

◆

The first athlete ever to win four gold medals in the Olympics was Jesse Owens—a Negro. Owens received medals for the 100-meter dash, the 200-meter dash, the broad jump, and for being a member of America's winning 400-meter relay team, in the 1936 games in Berlin. His spectacular achievements during those games infuriated Adolph Hitler and made ridiculous the Nazi myth of racial superiority. When Hitler refused to present him the medals he had won in the various competitions, Owens' fame became even more widespread as the result of the publicity.

Born on September 12, 1913, in Danville, Alabama, to sharecroppers who were so poor that they sometimes subsisted on potato peelings, Owens moved to Cleveland, Ohio, at an early age. In 1932, while attending East Technical High School in Cleveland, he gained national fame with a 10.3 clocking in the 100-meter dash. Two years later, Owens entered Ohio State University and for the next four years made track history. While competing in the Big Ten Championships at Ann Arbor, Michigan, on May 25, 1935, Owens had what has been called "the greatest single day in the history of man's athletic achievements." In the space of about seventy minutes, he tied the world record for the 100-yard dash and surpassed the world record for five other events, including the broad jump, the 220-yard low hurdles, and the 220-yard dash.

The first Negro women ever to win Olympic medals were two women who won medals in the Olympic Games in 1948 in London. Alice Coachman won a gold medal in the high jump, and Audrey Patterson won a bronze medal in track and field for the 200-meter run.

The first American woman to win three gold medals for running in the Olympics was Wilma Rudolph, a Negro. Representing the United States, she raced to fame at the 1960 Olympic Games. Wilma Rudolph, crippled by a childhood disease, had been unable to walk properly until she was eight years old. At twenty she was hailed as the "world's fastest woman."

Pan-African Congress

The first Pan-African Congress was convened by Dr. W. E. B. Du Bois in Paris, in 1921.

The Pan-African body began operation in 1917. Its purpose was to "establish some common meeting ground and unity of thought among the Negro people" of the whole world through biennial meetings of the Pan-African Congress. To use the words of the *Crisis*: "The problems of the American Negro must be thought of and settled only with continual reference to the problems of the West Indian Negroes, the problems of the French

Negroes and the English Negroes, and above all, the problems of the African Negroes. This is the thought of the Pan-African movement in all of its various manifestations."

Du Bois was awarded the Spingarn Medal on June 1, 1920, for the founding and convening of the Pan-African Congress.

Patent Office

The first Negro to work as a clerk in the U.S. Patent Office was Allen M. Bland, who received his appointment on April 12, 1869. Bland was one of the early Negro college graduates and was the father of James Bland, famous Negro composer of popular songs.

The first Negro appointed to a patent examiner position was Henry Edwin Baker. He was appointed on January 16, 1876. Baker was promoted through the years and ultimately achieved the position of Second Assistant Examiner. He retired on disability on April 7, 1925, after forty-nine years of service.

Mr. Baker was a cadet midshipman at the U.S. Naval Academy from June, 1874, until December, 1875. He attended law school and the Ben-Hyde School of Technology in Washington, D.C.

See also Inventions.

Penology

The first Negro in the country to head a major jail was Winston Moore, a black psychologist and former youth worker, who was appointed warden of Chicago's forty-year-old Cook County Jail in March, 1968. This jail was long regarded as a penal chamber of horrors. Juvenile delinquents were housed alongside crazed killers while awaiting trial. Homosexuality, drinking, beatings, and other social ills flourished there. At the time of his appointment Moore commented: "It'll take me a year to clean up this jail, and two years to gain full control." Since he has been there, Moore has fired fifty guards after they failed lie detector tests or were found with contraband which they were smuggling in and out of the prison. Those who stayed on were warned against brutality, required to learn the prisoners' names, and ordered to take a 96-hour police course in self-defense, sociology, and law.

Philanthropy

The first Negro philanthropist in the United States was Thomy Lafon, who was born in poverty in New Orleans in 1810. Through good sense and rare financial wisdom he amassed a personal fortune worth almost a half million dollars. A Catholic and a Negro, he generously left his life's earnings to Catholic and Protestant, black and white.

The following is part of a letter dated January 25, 1909, from Colonel James Lewis of New Orleans to Booker T. Washington, which gives valuable information about Thomy Lafon:

> The baptismal records in the archive of the Cathedral at that time written in Spanish attest that the late Mr. Thomy Lafon was born in this city on December 28th, 1810. He died at his home, corner Ursulines & Robertson Streets, on December 23rd, 1893, at the ripe age of 83 years. His body rests in the St. Louis cemetery on Esplanade Avenue. He was a man of dignified appearance and affable manners. In early life he taught school; later he operated a small dry goods store in Orleans Street until near into 1850. He was never married. Sometime before the war of Secession he had started his vast fortune by loaning money at advantageous rates of interest and by the accumulation of his savings. Toward the close of his career he became attached to the lamented Archbishop Janssens and began his philanthropies. By the terms of his will, dated April 3rd, 1890, he provided amply for his aged sister and some friends, and wisely distributed the bulk of his estate among public charitable institutions of New Orleans. His legacy was appraised at $413,000 divided in securities and realty.

In recognition of his charity, the city of New Orleans named one of its schools after Lafon.

Concerning his bust, which the state legislature ordered executed and placed in New Orleans, one commentator of that day noted: "It will be the first public testimonial by a state to a man of colour in recognition of his broad humanitarianism and true-hearted philanthropy."

Poetry

See Literature.

Police

The first known Negro police captain in America was Ocave Ray of the New Orleans Police Department. He had the reputation of knowing everyone in the city and never forgetting a face. Well-built, strong, and of courtly manners, he was one of the New Orleans major attractions. Captain Ray served from 1868 to 1877, and then was elected to the Louisiana State Legislature. He died in 1902, and was given a splendid public funeral.

◆

The first Negro detective sergeant of the New York City Police Force was Wesley Redding, who was promoted to that position in 1921.

◆

The first Negro Deputy Police Commissioner in the history of the City of New York was William L. Rowe. He was appointed to this position on August 23, 1951, by Mayor Vincent Impellitieri; Rowe remained in office until 1954.

◆

The first Negro officer to command a Harlem precinct was Captain Lloyd Sealy. His promotion as Captain in 1963 made him the holder of the highest post ever awarded a Negro in the New York City uniformed police. A native New Yorker, Sealy joined the force in 1942, later became a patrolman and sergeant in the Youth Division, and in 1959 was assigned to the Confidential Squad as a lieutenant.

◆

The first Negro Chief of Detectives for the police department of Springfield, Illinois, was Virgil L. Harvell, Sr., who was appointed in 1963, by Mayor Nelson O. Howarth on the recommendation of Chief Silver Suarez. Harvell, a veteran of twenty years with the department, became the highest ranking Negro police officer in any major city of the state.

In 1956, Harvell was the first Negro policeman to be appointed to the Civil Service classified position of sergeant.

◆

The first known Negro chief of police in the U.S. was Donald L. Colbert, thirty-nine, World War II Navy veteran, who in 1964 became the top law enforcement officer in Richmond, R.I., a town of nineteen hundred. Only four Negro families live in the town.

James N. Williams, executive secretary of the Urban League of Rhode Island, has observed that as far as he knows, Chief Colbert is the only Negro police chief in the country, with the possible exception of those in some all-Negro or predominantly Negro towns.

◆

The first Negro police major in the South was William Hughes, who was promoted to major in the Louisville, Kentucky, police department, in charge of the headquarters section, in 1965. According to Herbert T. Jenkins, Atlanta police chief and president of the International Association of Police Chiefs, no other police force in the South has a Negro in a position above lieutenant.

◆

The first county in the South to elect a Negro to the position of sheriff since reconstruction was Macon County, Alabama. Lucius D. Amerson, who twice attended law school to study law enforcement, was sworn in on January 3, 1967. He has hired three Negro and one white deputy.

The county has a population of twenty-seven thousand, 84 percent of whom are black—the highest ratio of blacks to whites of any county in the United States. In addition to the positions of sheriff, tax collector, and member of the board of education, Negroes occupy two of the five posts of the county commission, a majority of the police force in the major city, a majority of the county's jury lists posts on the city council, two of the four elective posts of the county commission, and a majority of the county's Democratic executive committee. Macon County and its principal city, Tuskegee, have perhaps the most integrated local governments in the United States today.

◆

The first Negro to head both the police and fire departments of a major American city was Lieutenant General Benjamin O. Davis, Jr., the highest-ranking Negro in the United States Armed Forces. He was appointed by Mayor Carl B. Stokes in 1970 to become the next safety director of Cleveland, Ohio. The appointment of the fifty-seven-year-old general, who was deputy commander of the U.S. Strike Command, coincided with his retirement from military service on February 1, after a distinguished thirty-seven-year military career.

Political Parties

The year 1940 represents the first time in this century that the Negro race was mentioned by name in a Democratic national platform. Part of the platform said, "Our Negro citizens have participated actively in the economic and social advances launched by this administration. . . . We shall continue to strive for complete legislative safeguards against discrimination in Government service and benefits, and in national defense forces. We pledge to uphold due process and the equal protection of laws for every citizen regardless of race, creed, or color."

Political Science

The first known Negro institution to have a Department of Political Science was Howard University, Washington, D.C. Dr. Ralph Bunche established this department in 1928. Prior to that the discipline was combined with history in the Department of History and Political Science.

The first Negro to receive a Ph.D. in political science was Ralph J. Bunche, Under-Secretary-General of the United Nations. Dr. Bunche received his degree from Harvard University in 1933.

The first Negro to head the American Political Science Association was Dr. Ralph J. Bunche, who held the office from 1953–54.

Post Office

The first Negro to hold a federal government post was William Cooper Nell, who was appointed postal clerk by the postmaster of Boston. Nell, who lived from 1816 to 1874, was primarily a writer and was known for his association with Frederick Douglass in publishing the *North Star*. Nell's other works include a pamphlet published in 1851, *Services of Colored Americans in the Wars of 1776 and 1812,* and *Colored Patriots of the American Revolution,* published in 1855, with an introduction written by Harriet Beecher Stowe.

◆

The first Negro to serve as postmaster in the United States was Henry McNeal Turner, who was appointed by President Grant as postmaster for Macon, Georgia, on May 18, 1869. He served through August 9, 1869 and resigned because of local political opposition.

◆

The first Negro to serve as postmistress in the United States was Minnie Cox who was appointed postmistress in the town of Indianola, Mississippi, by President Benjamin Harrison in 1890.

◆

The first Negro ever to head the post office of a major city was Leslie N. Shaw, who was appointed postmaster of Los Angeles, California, in 1963. His office has over ten thousand employees and does more than $84,000,000 annually in the sale of stamps and other services. Shaw received a B.S. degree from Ohio State University and is a graduate in business administration from UCLA.

Presbyterian Church

The first Negro Presbyterian Church was founded in 1807 in Philadelphia, Pennsylvania, with John Gloucester, an ex-slave, as its first pastor. It assumed the name First African, which it still holds today. The church grew out of the society at Keystone Hall, on 16th and Lombard streets. Moving to Seventh and Shippen streets (now Bainbridge Street), the congregation later moved to 17th and Fitzwater, and thence to 18th and Christian in 1943. The building at the latter address was condemned and demolished, and the congregation of First African Presbyterian now worships in its newest location at 42nd Street and Girard Avenue.

John Gloucester had been the body servant of Gideon Blackburn of Tennessee. Moved by his unusual gifts as a scholar and a preacher, his master liberated him so that he might engage in the ministry. Gloucester came to Philadelphia where he began his life's work as a missionary, exhorting from house to house. He then preached in a schoolhouse and finally had sufficient converts with whom to establish the First African Presbyterian Church in Philadelphia. Gloucester gave to that church four of his sons as ministers. He promoted the work of the church with unusual success until his death in 1822.

Presidents and the Negro

The first Negro to receive a major presidential appointment was Benjamin Banneker, the noted astronomer, mathematician, and linguist. In 1793, on the suggestion of Thomas Jefferson, President George Washington appointed Banneker to a commission of six men to lay the plans for the city of Washington. When the chairman, Major L'Enfant, suddenly resigned his position and left for France, he took all the layout plans with him. But Banneker's prodigious mind was able to reproduce them from memory. The physical design of Washington, D.C., stands today as a living monument to Benjamin Banneker's genius.

◆

The first Negro minister to preach a sermon on the death of a president was Richard Allen, the first black bishop in America and founder of the African Methodist Episcopal Church. On December 29, 1799, Allen gave a eulogy on Washington at Bethel Church. It was unusual for a Negro living at that time to be interested in public affairs to the extent that he would call the attention of the congregation to an outstanding event in a public address. He said in part:

> If he who broke the yoke of British burdens from the neck of the people of this land, was called his country's deliverer, by what name shall we call him who secretly and almost unknown emancipated his bondmen and bondwomen, and became to them a father, and gave them an inheritance? Deeds like these are not common. He did not let his right

hand know what his left hand did, but he who sees in secret rewards such acts of his beneficence. The name of Washington shall live when the sculptured marble and statue of bronze shall be crumbled into dust, for it is the decree of the eternal God that the righteous shall be held in everlasting remembrance, but the memorial of the wicked shall not.

◆

The first President to invite a Negro to dine at the White House was Thomas Jefferson, who, in 1805, invited Benjamin Banneker, the astronomer, mathematician, and linguist, to dine with him. The author of the immortal Declaration of Independence also invited Banneker to visit him at his home in Monticello, but the aged Negro was too feeble to travel and died the following year.

◆

The first known President to invite a Negro minister to conduct services at the White House was John Tyler (1841–45). He invited Bishop Payne of the African Methodist Episcopal Church to preach a funeral service over the coffin of his Negro body servant in a parlor of the presidential mansion. The Bishop remarked later that Tyler, in contrast to President Lincoln, had been stiff and formal.

◆

The first President to sign a charter establishing a Negro educational institution was Andrew Johnson, who, on March 2, 1867, signed into law the charter creating Howard University in Washington, D.C.

◆

The first President to appoint a Negro to represent the country abroad was Ulysses S. Grant, who, in 1869, appointed Ebenezer D. Bassett, an educator who studied at Yale, as American Resident and Consul General in Haiti.

◆

The first President to appoint a Negro postmaster was U.S. Grant, who appointed Henry McNeal Turner, the first Negro chaplain in the U.S. Army, to serve in Macon, Georgia, in 1869. A deputation of the first families of Georgia waited upon Grant to protest his ruling. The President replied that the appointment had been made and would stand. However, Turner resigned after serving in the post for only a few months because white racism prevented him from performing his duties.

◆

The first President invited to attend a civil rights meeting sponsored by Negroes was U. S. Grant. In answer to an invitation from a group of Washington, D.C., Negroes, he wrote the following letter:

> Executive Mansion
> Washington, D.C.
> May 9, 1872

Gentlemen:

I am in receipt of your invitation extended to me to attend a mass meeting, to be held for the purpose of aiding in securing civil rights for the colored citizens of our country. I regret that a previous engagement will detain me at the Executive Mansion this evening, and that I shall not be able to participate with you in person in your efforts to further the cause, in which you are laboring. I beg to assure you, however, that I sympathize most cordially in any effort to secure for all our people, of whatever race, nativity or color, the exercise of those rights to which every citizen should be entitled.

I am, very respectfully,

> U.S. Grant

◆

The first President to sign a civil rights bill was U. S. Grant. The Civil Rights Bill of 1875, as it was called, was supposed to secure to the Negro the privilege of riding in public conveyances, of entertainment at hotels, of attending the theater or places of amusement with no discrimination on account of color or previous condition of servitude. The last section of the bill granted the Negro the right to serve on juries. After passing both houses of Congress, the bill was signed by the President, and it became law on March 1, 1875.

◆

President Grant was probably the first and only Chief Executive ever to be arrested, and the arrest was made by a Negro policeman, William West. West was on duty at 12th and M Street in Washington, when he saw a horse and buggy coming toward him at furious speed. Reaching out he grabbed the bridle and stopped the horse. After being dragged half a block and recognizing the President, he apologized, but Grant insisted on being booked for breaking the law. West took him to the nearest police station. Grant had West promoted to mounted officer.

◆

The first known President to appoint a Negro as marshal was Rutherford B. Hayes, who, on March 15, 1877, appointed Frederick Douglass U.S. Marshal of the District of Columbia, marking the beginning of patronage jobs for Negroes.

◆

The first President known to visit a Negro school was Rutherford B. Hayes, who in September, 1877, visited the Central Colored School in Louisville, Kentucky. After music by the children was heard, the President praised the people of Louisville for their "liberal and just sentiments on the subject of education for all classes."

◆

The first President to appoint a Negro as Recorder of Deeds was James A. Garfield, who in 1881 appointed Frederick Douglass to this office for the District of Columbia.

◆

The first President to appoint a Negro as Registrar of the Treasury was James A. Garfield, who, in 1881, appointed to this high office Blanche K. Bruce, a former senator from Mississippi, the first Negro to serve a full term in the U.S. Senate. Bruce served a five-year period and was appointed to serve another term in 1898.

◆

The first Negro to be nominated as a presidential candidate at a Republican convention was Frederick Douglass, who received one vote at the 1888 Republican national convention in Chicago.

◆

The first President to recommend Congressional action to stop the crime of lynching was President Benjamin Harrison. In his last message to Congress, December 6, 1892, he recommended to Congress "repressive legislation" to stop the lynching of Negroes.

◆

The first President to appoint a Negro as minister to a white republic was Grover Cleveland, who, on September 5, 1893, appointed C. H. J. Taylor as Minister to Bolivia. The Afro-American Press meeting in Chicago on September 12 adopted a resolution endorsing President Cleveland's appointment of Taylor and asking the Senate to make a prompt confirmation. The Senate did not make the confirmation. Taylor accepted the post of Recorder of Deeds for the District of Columbia and held this position until his death on May 14, 1898.

◆

The first President to appoint a Negro to a sub-Cabinet post was William Howard Taft, who, in 1911, appointed William H. Lewis, a graduate of Amherst College and Harvard Law School, as Assistant Attorney General of the United States.

◆

The first President to appoint a Negro woman to a high executive post was Franklin D. Roosevelt, who, in 1936, appointed Dr. Mary McLeod Bethune as Director of Minority Affairs for the National Youth Administration.

◆

The first President in the history of the country to appoint a Negro to a federal judgeship was Franklin D. Roosevelt, who, in 1937, appointed Judge William H. Hastie to the U.S. District Court of the Virgin Islands.

◆

The first President to create a national committee on civil rights was Harry S Truman, in 1946.

◆

The first President to issue an executive order abolishing segregation in the armed forces was Harry S Truman, who, in 1948, issued this order.

◆

The first presidential inaugural ball in the history of the United States to which Negro citizens were invited as guests was held on January 20, 1949, at the beginning of the full term of President Harry S Truman.

◆

The first Negro to serve as chairman of the President's Committee on Government Employment Policy was Archibald J. Carey, who was appointed by President Dwight D. Eisenhower in 1957.

◆

The first President to appoint a Negro to a lifetime federal judgeship was John F. Kennedy. Other significant "firsts" scored by Kennedy included the appointments of A. Leon Higginbotham to the Federal Trade Commission in 1961, the first Negro appointed to a federal regulatory agency; Howard Jenkins, Jr., the first Negro member of the National Labor Relations Board in 1963; and Cecil F. Poole, the first Negro U.S. attorney who became U.S. attorney for Northern California in 1961.

◆

The first Negro to sit on the National Security Council was Carl T. Rowan, the former ambassador to Finland. In 1964, Rowan was appointed by President Lyndon Johnson as head of the U.S. Information Agency. The chief of this agency is automatically a member of the National Security Council.

◆

The first President to name a Negro to his Cabinet was Lyndon B. Johnson, who in 1966 nominated Robert C. Weaver, a Ph.D. in economics from Harvard University, as Secretary of Housing and Urban Development. Weaver served from January 18, 1966, to March 1, 1969.

◆

The first President to appoint a Negro to the United States Supreme Court was Lyndon B. Johnson, who, on June 12, 1967, named Thurgood Marshall to this high position.

Other significant "firsts" by President Johnson included the appointment of Major Hugh Robinson, the first black man to be named military presidential aide; Thurgood Marshall, the nation's first Negro Solicitor General; Walter Washington, the first Negro Mayor of Washington, D.C.; Barbara Watson, the first woman and the first Negro as Assistant Secretary of State; and Andrew F. Brimer, the first Negro to be appointed to the seven-man Federal Reserve Board.

◆

The first Negro nominated as a presidential candidate at a Democratic convention was the Reverend Channing Phillips, who received this honor at the 1968 Democratic National Convention in Chicago.

◆

The first Negro and the first twenty-eight year old ever nominated as Vice-President of the U.S. at a Democratic Convention was Julian Bond, member of the Georgia State Legislature. His name was put in nomination at the Democratic Convention in Chicago in 1968.

Bond was born in Nashville, Tennessee, on January 14, 1940. He attended primary school at Lincoln University in Pennsylvania, and was graduated from the George School, a coeducational Quaker preparatory school in Bucks County, Pa., June, 1957. He then entered Morehouse College in Atlanta, Georgia, where he immediately became involved in student organizations.

He was a founder of the Committee on Appeal for Human Rights, the Atlanta University Center student organization that coordinated three years of student antisegregation protests in Atlanta beginning in 1960. He served for three months as Executive Secretary of the COAHR. In April that year he helped to found the Student Nonviolent Coordinating Committee.

In January, the following year, he left Morehouse, just short of graduation, to serve as Communications Director of SNCC. In this capacity he went throughout the South participating in civil rights drives and voter registration campaigns.

Bond is a poet and essayist. His works have appeared in the *Negro Digest, Freedomways, Ramparts, New Negro Poets, American Negro Poetry, The Book of Negro Poetry,* and other publications.

After ten years as a dropout, Bond was awarded his B.A. degree at Morehouse in June, 1971.

The first black man to serve as presidential aide in the White House was E. Frederick Morrow, who was appointed by President Richard M. Nixon in 1969.

The first Negro named to the National Highway Safety Advisory Committee was Dr. Basil Scott of East Greenbush, New York. He was appointed by President Nixon in January, 1970. The NHSA Committee, created by Congress under the Highway Act of 1966, is composed of thirty-five members, each with a tenure of three years.

Dr. Scott was born in Barbados, British West Indies, on January 18, 1925. He is a graduate of City College of New York in 1948, having received his B.A. in economics and statistics. He was awarded an M.B.A. degree from Siena College in Tennessee in economics and accounting, and a D.P.A. from Syracuse University in public administration.

In his present position Dr. Scott serves as the Deputy Administrative Director for the New York State Department of Motor Vehicles.

The first Negro member of the Federal Trade Commission was A. Leon Higginbotham, who was appointed in 1970.

Higginbotham was born in Trenton, New Jersey, in 1927. After studying at Purdue University and Antioch College, he enrolled at Yale and received his LL.B. in 1952.

He was soon appointed assistant district attorney in Philadelphia; then he joined a private law firm and, later, was chosen by Pennsylvania's Governor David Lawrence to serve as a member of the Pennsylvania Human Rights Commission.

The first deceased Negro to be eulogized by a President at graveside services was Whitney M. Young, Jr. On March 17, 1971, President Richard Nixon came to the Bluegrass section of Kentucky to pay tribute to a deceased friend and renowned leader, Whitney M. Young, Jr., former head of the National Urban League.

This President observed that Whitney Young was a "doer, not a talker . . . and at a time when so many asked what can the government do, he stood up and said, 'What can I do? What can I do to make the American Dream come true?' Whitney Young's genius was—he knew how to accomplish what other people merely were for . . . He leaves his own monument—not one, but thousands . . . Thousands of men and women in his own race will have a chance, an equal chance, who otherwise might never have had a chance except for what he did. And thousands of others not of his own race, who have an understanding in their hearts which they would not have had except for what he taught."

See also Judges.

Psychology

The first Negro to receive a Ph.D. in psychology was Francis Cecil Sumner. Clark University of Worcester, Massachusetts, awarded him this degree in 1920. The title of his doctoral dissertation was *Psychoanalysis of Freud and Adler.*

Dr. Sumner was born in Pine Bluff, Arkansas, on December 7, 1895. He received his A.B. from Clark University in Georgia in 1915, and his M.A. from Lincoln University in 1916. He has served as instructor of German and psychology at Lincoln University; professor of psychology and philosophy at Wilberforce University; and professor of psychology and head of the department of psychology at Howard University.

◆

The first Negro to be elected president of the seventy-seven-year-old American Psychological Association was Dr. Kenneth B. Clark, a noted psychologist and author of books on minority status and desegregation problems. He assumed office as president of the APA, which has about 28,500 members, in October, 1970. Clark is currently a professor of psychology at the City College of the City University of New York, president of the Metropolitan Applied Research Center, and the only black member of the New York State Board of College Regents. His studies on Negro and white children were considered by the U.S Supreme Court in making the 1954 *Brown* decision. Dr. Clark is a trustee of Howard University and recently resigned as trustee of Antioch College in Ohio after the college inaugurated a black studies program that he believed to be separatist in nature.

Radio

The first Negro disc jockey was Jack L. Cooper. He began his broadcasting career in 1923, over radio station WCAP in Washington, D.C. His shows emanated from the Wardman Park Hotel, which like other major Washington facilities at that time, engaged in racial discrimination. "Negroes weren't even allowed in the back door there," Cooper told a *Daily Defender* interviewer in 1963, "but I changed all of that!"

Cooper died in January, 1970.

◆

The first Negro radio station to go on the air was WERD, operating out of Atlanta, Georgia. WERD began broadcasting in 1949.

◆

The established Negro radio network was the National Negro Network, formed on January 20, 1954. The first program was *The Story of Ruby Valentine,* starring Juanita Hall, broadcast on January 25, 1954, on forty stations. The program was sponsored five days a week alternately by Philip Morris & Co., Ltd., and Pet Milk Company. The New York City outlet of the station was WOV.

Resettlement

The first effort at resettlement of Africa by Americans was made by Paul Cuffe, a Negro ship captain and merchant. He made his living by hauling cargo to different parts of the world. In 1811, Cuffe sailed one of his ships, the *Traveller,* from Massachusetts to Sierra Leone, Africa, where he founded the Friendly Society for the emigration of free Negroes from America. The War of 1812 interrupted his colonization plans but in 1815 he took thirty-eight Negroes to Sierra Leone at a cost of $4,000 from his personal funds. Cuffe planned many more trips with black colonists, but his health failed; he died in 1817.

◆

The first President of Liberia was Joseph Jenkins Roberts, who was born in America in 1809, but emigrated to Liberia in 1829 with his mothers and brothers. After establishing himself as a merchant, he became president of the colony in 1842. Roberts was responsible for achieving Liberia's status as a sovereign and independent republic in 1847. He was reelected president of the republic in 1849, 1851, and 1853. After eighteen years out of office, Roberts was again elected president in 1871, and served in that office until his death in 1876.

◆

The first Negro to form a nationwide back-to-Africa movement was Marcus Garvey. Black Zionism was not new in America, but it had never before attracted such a mass following. Garvey has been called the leader of the first great mass movement among blacks.

Marcus Garvey was born at St. Ann's Bay, Jamaica, about 1885. He was educated at the public school and then for a short time attended the Church of England Grammar School, although he was a Roman Catholic. On leaving school he learned the printing trade and followed it for many years.

Arriving in the United States in 1916, he organized the Universal Negro Improvement Association (UNIA) and started a steamship line, the Black Star Line, in connection with his mission. His motto was "Africa for the Africans." He instilled pride in the African heritage, maintaining that Europe was inhabited by savages while Africa was peopled with a race of cultured black men. "Black men you were once great; you shall be great again."

Garvey praised everything black and was suspicious of everything white. He formed the Universal Black Cross Nurses, the Black Church, the Black Star Line, the Universal African Motor Corps, and the Black Flying Eagles.

While millions followed him without hesitation, Negro intellectuals, led by W. E. B. Du Bois, were skeptical of Garvey and his promises. They felt that his plans were far too impracticable and fantastic. In 1925, Garvey was imprisoned for using the mails to defraud in connection with the sale of stock in his Black Star Line, and his dream began to fade. After serving two years in prison, he was deported from America and died in London in 1940, a lonely and penniless man.

Rhodes Scholars

The first Negro to win a Rhodes scholarship was Alain L. Locke of Pennsylvania. He attended Oxford University from 1907 to 1910. He received his A.B. degree from Harvard College in 1908, and his Ph.D. in philosophy in 1917, from Harvard University. Dr. Locke was elected to Phi Beta Kappa at Harvard, and later he led a successful move to establish a Phi Beta Kappa at Howard University, where he taught for forty-one years.

In the area of philosophy, Locke's writings have been regarded as "original contributions in a highly controversial field." His philosophical works include *The Problem of Classification, Theory of Value and Values,* and *Imperatives in American Philosophy: Today and Tomorrow.*

Dr. Locke was the first to edit an anthology of Afro-American drama, *Plays of Negro Life* (1927). Some of his other works were *The New Negro, The Negro in America, The Negro and His Music, Negro Art—Past and Present,* and *The Negro in Art.*

Dr. Locke was the first Negro to be elected president of the National Council of Adult Education. He was an exchange professor to Haiti in 1943, and a visiting professor at several universities, including Fisk, New York University, and the University of Wisconsin.

At the time of his death in 1954, he was working on a book entitled *The Negro in American Culture.* This book was completed by Margaret Just Butcher.

Roman Catholic Church

The first Negro Catholic nuns (Colored Community) were the Oblate Sisters of Providence, founded by Jacques Hector Nicholas Joubert de la Muraille on July 2, 1829, in Baltimore, Maryland. Pope Gregory XVI approved the order on October 2, 1831.

The first Catholic parish church for Negroes was St. Francis Xavier's, in Baltimore, Maryland, which was purchased on October 10, 1863, and dedicated on February 21, 1864.

The first Negro Catholic priest ordained to work in the United States was the Reverend Augustus Tolton. He was born in Ralls County, Missouri, but had grown up in Quincy, Illinois, where his mother had taken him after escaping from slavery. A devout Catholic, Tolton was encouraged in his studies by his priests and bishops and, when he was sure of his true vocation, they helped him to secure admission to the College of Propaganda in Rome, Italy, in 1880. After mastering this course of study, Augustus Tolton was ordained a priest on Holy Saturday, April 24, 1886.

On Easter Sunday in 1886, this black priest offered Holy Mass on the High Altar at St. Peter's Basilica in Rome. As a rule only the Pope himself offers Mass over the tomb of Saint Peter; but this was no ordinary occasion. Instead, it was the Church's way of honoring the first full-blooded American Negro ever to be ordained for the priesthood.

Returning to Quincy, Illinois, in the summer of 1886, Father Tolton assumed the pastorship of St. Joseph's Catholic Church for Negroes—a very small church. In 1889, a wealthy individual donated $10,000 for the establishment of St. Monica's Church for Negro Catholics in Chicago. In 1890, the church was ready for service, and Father Tolton served as pastor for seven years. He died on July 10, 1897.

◆

The first national convention of Negro Catholics, composed of delegates from nearly all the Negro Catholic churches and societies throughout the country, was held in Washington, D.C., for three days, January 8–10, 1889. Father Tolton of Quincy, Illinois, the only Negro priest in the United States, began the celebration of solemn high mass. Cardinal Gibbons delivered the main sermon in which he said, "This gathering will mark an era in the history of the colored people of the United States, for never before have Colored Catholics of the country met in convention." Temporary organization was effected by choosing William H. Smith as its first president.

◆

The first Catholic seminary for the education of Negro priests was opened by the missionaries of the Society of the Divine Word, at Bay St. Louis, Mississippi, and was dedicated on September 16, 1923.

◆

The first Negro ever consecrated as a bishop of the Roman Catholic Church for the United States was the Most Reverend Harold Perry.

Bishop Perry was born in Lake Charles, Louisiana, in 1916. Since his ordination he has served as assistant pastor in Immaculate Heart of Mary Parish, Lafayette, Louisiana; Saint Peter's Parish, Pine Bluff, Arkansas; Saint Gabriel's Parish, Mound Bayou, Mississippi; and Our Lady of Perpetual Help Parish, Saint Martinville, Louisiana. In 1958, he was appointed rector of Saint Augustine Seminary at Bay St. Louis, Mississippi.

The prelate is a man of many "firsts." In 1963, he became the first Negro to deliver the invocation at an opening session of the U.S. Congress. In 1964, he was appointed Provincial Superior of the Southern Province of the Divine Word Seminaries, covering eleven states of the Old Confederacy—the first Negro major Religious Superior of men in the United States. In a surprise move, late in 1965, Pope Paul VI named Monsignor Perry Auxiliary Bishop to Archbishop Philip M. Hanan of the New Orleans Archdiocese. Hanan, in turn, made Perry America's Negro Vicar General, equal in rank to his other auxiliary, Bishop L. Abel Caillouet. Before his consecration in January, 1966, in St. Louis Basilica in New Orleans, Bishop Perry had felt surprised at being assigned to New Orleans, but later he saw the wisdom of the choice, he asserted, because, "Louisiana has the largest concentration of Negro Catholics in the United States, some 200,000. I think it is complimentary to the deep Catholic faith of all the people in New Orleans that the Holy See chose this city."

◆

The first Negro from the Americas to be made a saint was Martin de Porres of Lima, Peru. In May, 1962, in St. Peter's in Rome, some thirty thousand persons stood in silence as Pope John XXIII proclaimed Peruvian Negro monk, Martin de Porres, a saint.

Martin de Porres was born in a wretched hut in Lima, Peru, on December 9, 1579, the illegitimate son of Don Juan de Porres of Burgois, an adventuring Spanish noble, and Ana Velasque, a former Negro slave. At the time there was racial inequality between the intruding Spanish, the native Indians, and the imported African slaves. Brother Martin built a bridge of charity and understanding between the races, not by writing about social justice but by practicing it.

Brother Martin ranks high among the church's spectacular healers of the sick and comforters of the afflicted. As the convent's almoner, he gave away more than $2,000 a week in food and clothing to Lima's poor. Placed in charge of the Dominican Infirmary, he filled up the beds with derelicts whom he found lying in the streets. Before he died in 1639, Brother Martin had established an orphanage and foundling hospital. He loved animals as well as people and filled the convent with wounded stray dogs and cats, which he nursed back to health.

Famed in his own lifetime for his miraculous cures of the dying, Brother Martin was venerated by Limenos as a potential saint almost from the day of his death. He was beatified by Pope Gregory XVI in 1827, an honor which carries the title "blessed" and is sometimes the first step to canonization. Pope Pius XI opened the investigation of his life in 1926, after devotion to him had spread outside Peru to the U.S. and Africa.

The official Vatican account of his sanctity notes: "By his whole apostolic life, his prayers, his words, his example, even his miracles, he made it clear that every race and nationality has the same dignity, the same equality, because we are all sons of one heavenly Father and redeemed by Christ the Lord."

Salvation Army

The first black Salvation Army Lieutenant Colonel in the U.S. was B. Barton McIntyre. General Erik Wickberg, the international leader of the Salvation Army, announced McIntyre's promotion in 1970, thus making him the highest ranking black Salvation Army officer in the U.S. His current position is Territorial Revivalist for the Salvation Army in eleven Eastern states.

Lieutenant Colonel McIntyre has been an officer in the Salvation Army for thirty-eight years, during which time he has served the organization in appointments at Brooklyn, New York, Cleveland, Ohio, and in the Harlem section of New York City. Prior to his present assignment he served as Divisional Secretary for the metropolitan New York district, an executive position involving the supervision and coordination of Salvation Army activities in thirty units of service within the metropolitan area. He has served as counselor on minority relations in Washington, D.C., St. Louis, Chicago, Cleveland, Ohio, and Memphis, Tennessee.

Lieutenant Colonel McIntyre holds the bachelor of theology degree from Malone College in Canton, Ohio. He has studied at the College of the City of New York, Oberlin College, the Shauffler School of Social Sciences, and Cleveland Bible College.

Science

The first Negro to receive the Spingarn Medal from the NAACP was Ernest Just for his outstanding research in biology. This honor came to him on February 12, 1915, at Ethical Culture Hall in New York City. The late Dr. Charles Drew described Just as a "biologist of unusual skill and the greatest of our original thinkers in the field." He was seen as producing "new concepts of cell life and metabolism which will make for him a place for all time."

Born of middle-class parents in 1883, in Charleston, South Carolina, Just attended Dartmouth College, graduating magna cum laude and with Phi Beta Kappa honors. Later he was Howard University's outstanding professor in the biological sciences and received many awards and grants for his research. Scientists from all over America and Europe sought him out and studied his work. Just developed an interest in marine biology in the study of which he spent several years at the University of Chicago while carrying on his research at Woods Hole, Massachusetts. He obtained there the degree of Doctor of Philosophy in 1916.

Dr. Just wrote two major books, *The Biology of the Cell Surface,* 1939, and *Basic Methods for Experiments on Eggs of Marine Animals,* 1939, and over sixty scientific papers in his field. He died in 1941.

The first Negro to obtain a Ph.D. degree in chemistry was St. Elmo Brady. His degree was awarded by the University of Illinois in 1916.

Dr. Percy L. Julian represents, perhaps, our first contributor to fundamental knowledge in pure chemistry in this country. In 1935, Dr. Julian synthesized and made in pure form for the first time, physostigmine, a myotic alkaloid from the calabar bean. This drug had been used in treating certain severe abdominal conditions by physicians for many years but it had never been prepared synthetically in its pure state, although a professor at the University of London had worked on the problem for more than twenty years with no apparent success.

Julian's mastery of the chemistry of the soya bean has led to the preparation of such widely different substances as a male sex hormone and a weatherproof covering for a battleship. Dr. Julian is credited with the saving of thousands of American seamen and airmen during World War II, as a result of his development of a new soya protein, which formed the basis for the navy's sensational Aero-Foam. Many of our warships, and particularly our aircraft carriers, survived the grueling Pacific fighting as a result of the development of this product which was used to extinguish gasoline and other types of fires where a smothering agent is necessary.

Dr. Julian was born of impoverished parents in Alabama. He graduated from DePauw University in Indiana at the head of his class and was awarded a scholarship to Harvard University. At Harvard, he was awarded the highest honors and then received a scholarship to Vienna University, where he also led his graduating class. He received the Ph.D. degree in chemistry at Vienna. Before going to Glidden Corporation as director of research, Dr. Julian taught chemistry at Fisk and West Virginia State University.

Dr. Julian received the Spingarn Medal from the NAACP in 1947 for the highest achievement made by a Negro-American that year. Dr. Louis T. Wright wrote in the citation: "This medal is presented in recognition of his work as a distinguished chemist who has made many important discoveries that have saved many lives. He has demonstrated skill, courage, and sustained effort on the highest level in making contributions that will benefit mankind in years to come. The world will pay tribute to his efforts in behalf of the welfare of humanity."

In accepting the award, Dr. Julian called on scientists "to bring to the world a living testimony from the pages of science against a philosophy of defeatism," and to "hold out to the world the hope of peace."

Dr. Julian is currently Director of the Julian Research Institute, in Franklin Park, Illinois.

◆

The first Negro scientist to have a monument dedicated to him was George Washington Carver; the monument was dedicated on July 14, 1955, near Diamond, in southwest Missouri.

Born of slave parents in 1864, in Diamond Grove, Missouri, Carver was only an infant when he and his mother were abducted from his owner's plantation by a band of slave raiders. His mother was sold and shipped away, but her son was ransomed by his master in exchange for a race horse valued at $300. The boy—was physically frail—was returned to the plantation of George and Susan Carver in Missouri where he was to be reared.

Carver's early training was in a small, one-room school at Neosho, Missouri, about eight miles from the Carver plantation. He continued his education in Minneapolis, Kansas, where he received a high school diploma. After being turned down by Highland College in Kansas, he was finally admitted as the first Negro student at Simpson College in Indianola, Iowa, where he studied art and piano. The following year he was transferrred to the State Agricultural College at Ames, Iowa, and received the bachelor's and master's degrees in agriculture from Iowa State College in 1894 and 1896, respectively.

In 1896, Dr. Carver (who had received an honorary Doctor of Science degree from the University of Rochester) was on the faculty of Iowa State College as its first Negro teacher when he accepted the invitation of Booker T. Washington to join the faculty of Tuskegee Normal and Industrial Institute in Alabama. He began his work at Tuskegee on October 8 of that year as director of the department of agriculture. He served also as director of the Agricultural Experiment Station, which had been authorized for Tuskegee by the Alabama legislature.

Carver's investigations yielded nearly three hundred products from the peanut, one hundred from the sweet potato, and scores of others from Alabama's red clay. An authority on plant diseases, especially the fungus variety, Dr. Carver sent hundreds of specimens to the U.S. Department of Agriculture.

Dr. Carver died on January 5, 1946, at Tuskegee, where he was buried on the campus near the grave of Booker T. Washington, the school's founder.

In 1956, Simpson College dedicated a new science building in his honor.

◆

The first Negro appointed to the United States Atomic Energy
Commission was Dr. Samuel Nabrit. He was nominated for a
four-year term by President Lyndon B. Johnson and was sworn in
at the White House on August 1, 1966, on the twentieth anniversary of the signing of the Atomic Energy Act.

Born on February 21, 1905, in Macon, Georgia, Nabrit
moved with his family to Augusta, where he attended Walker
Baptist Institute. He continued his education at Morehouse College, earning his B.A. in 1925. In 1932, he won the distinction of
being the first Negro to earn a Ph.D. from Brown University.
President of Texas Southern University since 1955, Nabrit previously served as dean of the Graduate School of Arts and Sciences
at Atlanta University, where he was a member of the faculty for
nearly a quarter-century.

Sculpture

The first Negro sculptor to achieve distinction in a field
generally dominated by white men was Edmonia Lewis, who was
born in 1845, in Greenhigh, Ohio. She was the daughter of a
Chippewa Indian mother and a free Negro father. She was
orphaned at an early age and brought up first by Indian kinsmen
and then at an orphanage until sent by a group of abolitionists to
Oberlin College, the first American institution of higher learning to
admit women on a nonsegregated basis. Subsequently, William
Lloyd Garrison brought her to the attention of the Boston sculptor,
Edmund Brackett, who trained her until she was sent to Rome for
further instructions by white patrons, the Story family.

Her best known works include *Hiawatha, The Marriage of
Hiawatha, Hagar in the Wilderness, Madonna and Child, Forever
Free,* and *The Death of Cleopatra.* She also did a bust of Henry
Wadsworth Longfellow for the Harvard College Library.

Miss Lewis died in Rome in 1890.

◆

The first and only Negro sculptor to become a member of the
National Academy of Arts and Letters was Richard Barthe, who
was born in 1901 in Bay St. Louis, Mississippi. Barthe began his
training as a painter with study at the Chicago Art Institute. In

1929, he received a Rosenwald grant, which enabled him to continue his training in New York City. His works were bought by the Whitney Museum in New York as well as by other prominent galleries, and he has had several one-man shows in New York. In 1946, Barthe was commissioned to sculpt the bust of Booker T. Washington, which was eventually placed in New York University's Hall of Fame.

Selective Service System

The first black state director of Selective Service was Ernest D. Fears. He was appointed to the post by Governor Linwood Holton, who promised to make Virginia "a model of race relations." He assumed his duties on January 1, 1971.

Fears was given a leave of absence by predominantly black Norfolk State College, where he is athletic director and physical education instructor. His office staff in Richmond, Virginia, consists of five military officers and nineteen civilians, supervising the operation of 129 local draft boards across the commonwealth.

Fears received his B.A. degree from Florida A & M University and a master's degree from Ohio State University. At Florida A & M he captained the basketball team for three years and played on three conference championship teams.

Sit-Ins

No one knows precisely when the first sit-in took place. The eminent Negro historian, Benjamin Quarles, states: "Strictly speaking the sit-in technique is not new. Since Reconstruction days Negroes have protested segregation by taking seats in white sections of theaters and streetcars."

◆

The first sit-in demonstration organized by the Committee on Racial Equality (CORE) took place at a restaurant in the Loop area of Chicago, Illinois, in 1943.

◆

The first sit-in demonstration to take place in the Deep South occurred in 1960 at the Montgomery, Alabama, courthouse. The demonstration was organized by students from Alabama State

College, nine of whom were later suspended by the State Board of Education for their participation in the sit-in.

The first sit-in to become a national movement began on February 1, 1960, at the F. W. Woolworth lunch counter in Greensboro, North Carolina. It was begun by four freshmen engineering students (Franklin McCain, Joseph McNeal, David Richmond, and Ezelle Vlair, Jr.) from North Carolina A & T College. The four sat at the counter and continued to sit there until the store closed. The group returned the next day with reinforcements, and the sit-in movement was on its way. It captured the imagination of eager blacks in the South of 1960, and gave them a nonviolent means of protesting the many injustices they felt they had been dealt.

McCain said none of the four envisioned his sit-in protest at Woolworth's becoming a national movement. "It was just an idea whose time had come," he said. "It was ripe. The timing was right."

McNeal said, "Looking back, it seems that the sit-in not only removed the barriers of public accommodations in Greensboro, but was the impetus for passing the public accommodations law on a national scale."

See also Civil Rights.

Slavery

The first Negroes in English America were twenty who were brought to Jamestown, Virginia, by a Dutch man-of-war in 1619 as indentured servants—a condition which inevitably led to slavery. Hence, with their landing, the racial problem with which we are directly concerned began.

The first state to legally recognize slavery was Massachusetts, which in 1641 had its "Body of Liberties" sanction slavery by providing that there was not to be bond slavery in the colony "unless it be lawful Captives taken in just warres, and such strangers as willingly sell themselves or are sold to us."

Virginia gave statutory recognition to slavery in 1661. By the end of the century, Negro slavery was an accepted and important part of colonial life.

◆

The first recorded slave revolt occurred in Gloucester, Virginia, in 1663, and such uprisings continued throughout the slavery era. Dwight Dummond, the foremost authority on slavery, states, "There were a score of recorded insurrections of some magnitude in colonial days: in New York, in Charleston, in New Orleans, and in various rural communities from Maryland to Georgia." The 250 revolts reported involved numbers ranging from 10 to 50,000 slaves.

◆

The first American letter against slavery was written on August 4, 1776, by Henry Laurens, a wealthy South Carolina merchant who was a member of the Continental Congress at that time, to his son John Laurens. He defended his belief that Negro slaves were entitled to the "unalienable rights" set forth in the Declaration of Independence, just adopted. This letter is now in the archives of Columbia University in New York.

◆

The first emancipated slave was Elizabeth Freeman, owned by Colonel Ashley of Sheffield, Massachusetts, in 1780. Mrs. Ashley endeavored to strike Elizabeth's sister with a red hot poker. Elizabeth interfered, received the blow instead, and ran away. In a trial in Great Barrington, Massachusetts, Judge Theodore Sedgwick of Stockbridge, Massachusetts, upheld her and granted her freedom.

◆

The first state law abolishing slavery was "an act for the gradual abolition of slavery," passed by the Pennsylvania legislature on March 1, 1780.

◆

The first organization to come out openly against slavery was the Society of Friends, a Quaker group. By 1787, no Quaker owned slaves.

◆

The first antislavery pamphlet by a Negro was published in 1789. It was entitled *On Slavery*. The author was a Negro freeman who hid his identity under the pen name "Othello." It is conjectured that he was the mathematician and astronomer Benjamin Banneker, who, in 1791, addressed a long letter in similar vein to Thomas Jefferson.

◆

The first Underground Railroad began during the 1820's, and was manned by Negroes and white abolitionists who provided for the conveyance of escaped slaves to the free territories and Canada. Between 1830 and 1860, it helped no less than 75,000 slaves to find freedom. The most famous of all Underground Railroad operators was undoubtedly Harriet Tubman.

◆

The first federal fugitive slave law was passed on February 12, 1793. It provided for the return of fugitives from justice and from labor: "No person held to service of labor in one state under the laws thereof escaping into another, shall be delivered up on claim of the party to whom such service or labor may be due."

◆

The first antislavery magazine was a monthly, *The Emancipator,* issued from April 30, 1820, to October 31, 1820. It was edited and published by Elilu Embree in Jonesboro, Tennessee.

◆

The first antislavery book was published in Boston in 1833 by Allen & Ticknor. It was written by Lydia Maria Francis Child, and entitled *An Appeal in Favor of That Class of Americans Called Africans.*

◆

The first Negro to take the platform as a regular lecturer in the antislavery cause was Charles L. Remond. He was the ablest representative that the black race had until the appearance of Frederick Douglass in 1842.

◆

The first antislavery party was the Liberty Party, which held its first convention in Warsaw, New York, on November 13, 1839.

The first national convention of the Liberty Party was held in New York City on May 12, 1840. The party nominated Gillespie Birney, a former slaveholder of a deeply religious bent, for the presidency and Francis Julius LeMoyne for the vice-presidency. In the Harrison-Van Buren election in 1840 the candidates polled 7,069 votes.

The new party entered the lists in the next election in 1844, holding its national convention in Buffalo. The presence of three famous abolitionists, Henry Highland Garnet, Samuel Ringgold Ward, and Charles Ray was significant—never before in America had Negroes been active in the councils of a political party. In the presidential election of that year the Liberty Party, again headed by Birney, increased its popular vote to 62,263.

After 1844 the Liberty Party lost strength because of its preoccupation with a single issue. Voters wanted the party to assume a position on the tariff, the bank, the distribution of lands, and the annexation of Texas.

See also Abolitionism.

Sociology

. The first sociological study of the Northern urban Negro written by a Negro was *Sketches of the Higher Classes of Colored Society in Philadelphia,* published in 1841. Although the author remained anonymous, his race was referred to in the book itself.

The first real sociological research in the South, according to Guy Johnson, was done by the Conference on Negro Problems held annually at Atlanta University between 1896 and 1914 under the general direction of W. E. B. Du Bois. Among the more valuable publications of the conference were *Some Efforts of Negroes for Social Betterment* (1898), *The Negro in Business* (1899), *The College-bred Negro* (1900), and *The Common School* (1901).

The first known doctorate in sociology earned by a Negro was conferred on Richard Robert Wright, Jr., in 1911, by the University of Pennsylvania. His thesis was entitled "The Negro in Pennsylvania—A Study in Economic History." He operated a bookshop in

Philadelphia. Richard Robert Wright later became a bishop in the African Methodist Church.

◆

The first black man to be appointed visiting professor of sociology at New York University was Dr. Ira Reid in 1946. He also has served as chairman of the department of sociology and anthropology at Haverford College in Pennsylvania. His books and monographs on interracial problems are highly regarded by sociologists around the country. Some of the most noted ones include *Negro Immigrant, In a Minor Key, Adult Education Among Negroes, Negro Membership in American Labor Unions, Urban Negro Workers in the U.S., 1924–35,* and, with Arthur Raper as coauthor, *Sharecroppers All.* Before joining the Haverford faculty, Dr. Reid taught at Atlanta University, where he was an associate of Du Bois. The two worked together on the founding of *Phylon,* the school's quarterly review of race and culture, and Dr. Reid succeeded Dr. Du Bois as editor in 1943. Dr. Reid also served as director of research for the National Urban League. Reid died in 1968 at Bryn Mawr Hospital in Philadelphia after a long illness.

◆

The first Negro to head the Southern Sociological Society was Dr. Charles Spurgeon Johnson of Fisk University, one of the most eminent black sociologists of his generation. He served as President of this distinguished organization for the 1946–47 fiscal year.

The sociological observations recorded by Dr. Johnson about mankind and its institutions and problems now fill eighteen books. One of them, *The Negro in Chicago,* is considered a landmark in social research. Among his other books are *Patterns of Negro Segregation, The Negro in American Civilization, Negro Housing, Economic Status of the Negro, Shadow of the Plantation, Collapse of Cotton Tenancy, Growing Up in the Black Belt, Into the Mainstream,* and *Education and the Cultural Crisis.*

◆

The first American Negro elected president of the American Sociological Society was internationally known Dr. E. Franklin Frazier, in 1948. A year later he was named Chairman of UNESCO's committee of experts on race. Later he served as chief of UNESCO's Applied Science Division in Paris.

Born in Baltimore in 1894, Frazier graduated from Howard University in 1916, and received his Ph.D. from the University of Chicago in 1931. In 1934, he began a twenty-five year period of service in the sociology department at Howard. A student of Negro life, he wrote *The Black Bourgeois, The Negro Family, On Race Relations, The Negro in the United States,* and *The Negro Church.*

On September 8, 1956, Frazier received the MacIver Lectureship Award of the American Sociological Society, granted annually to the sociologist "who had contributed outstandingly in the progress of sociology by his published or unpublished works." The award was for Professor Frazier's book, *Bourgeoisie Noir,* a historical analysis of Negro life in the United States. The presentation was at the dinner marking the annual meeting of the society.

Frazier died in 1963 at George Washington University hospital after a long illness. He had retired from Howard in 1959.

Sororities

The first Negro sorority was Alpha Kappa Alpha, founded on January 15, 1908, at Howard University in Washington, D.C., by Ethel Hedgeman Lyle. The first officers were Lucy Slowe, president; Ethel Hedgeman Lyle, vice-president; Marie Woolfolk, secretary; and Anna Brown, treasurer. On January 29, 1913, the sorority was incorporated in the District of Columbia.

Southern Christian Leadership Conference (SCLC)

The founder and first head of the Southern Christian Leadership Conference was Martin Luther King, Jr., who organized the conference in March, 1957. Its stated purpose is to achieve full citizenship rights and the integration of the Negro in all aspects of life. The technique of the organization is the use of the philosophy of nonviolence as a means of creative protest and voter registration drives. The famous March on Washington in 1963, led by SCLC, resulted in the passage of the Civil Rights Act of 1964.

Martin Luther King, Jr., was born in 1929, in Atlanta, Georgia. He attended the local Booker T. Washington High School, studied at Morehouse College, and under the influence of its famed president emeritus, Dr. Benjamin E. Mayes, entered the ministry in 1947. King graduated from Morehouse in 1948, and in

1951 he received the B.D. degree from Crozer Theological Seminary, where he was an excellent student. In 1955, he earned the Ph.D. degree from Boston University.

Martin Luther King's broad public career and the black "revolt" began together on December 1, 1955, when Rosa Parks, a Montgomery seamstress, refused to yield her bus seat to a white male as required by the laws and customs of Alabama, and was arrested. Within five days after her arrest, the blacks organized the Montgomery Improvement Association and elected the Reverend Martin Luther King, Jr., president. He organized a successful boycott which terminated segregation on buses in Montgomery.

Dr. King received the Nobel Peace Prize in Oslo, Norway, on December 10, 1964. At thirty-five, he became the youngest man in history to receive this coveted distinction. For the first time a degree of official international recognition was connected with his struggle. There was a sense that the nonviolent aspects of the civil rights struggle had captured global attention.

His assassination on April 4, 1968, in Memphis, Tennessee, while aiding the cause of the striking garbage collectors in that city, became, in the opinion of many, the force that led to the Civil Rights Act of 1968.

Sports

See Baseball; Basketball; Bowling; Boxing; Golf; Horse Racing; Olympics; Tennis.

Stamps

The first U.S. stamp to honor a Negro pictures Booker T. Washington. Valued at ten cents, the stamp belongs to the Famous Americans series. It went on sale at Tuskegee Institute on April 7, 1940.

The first U.S. stamp to honor a Negro scientist was that of Dr. George Washington Carver. It went on sale at Tuskegee Institute on January 5, 1948.

The first Negro to design a U.S. postage stamp was George Olden, internationally known in graphic arts. He designed the Emancipation Proclamation stamp, which went on sale on August 16, 1963, in Chicago, Illinois.

◆

The first U.S. stamp to honor a Negro civil rights leader was that of Frederick Douglass. It went on sale on February 14, 1967, at the Frederick Douglass Institute of Negro Arts and History in Washington, D.C. It was a $.25 stamp issued as the eighth in a new series of eighteen regular stamps to be known as the Prominent Americans series.

Frederick Douglass is regarded by black scholars as the greatest Negro of the last century. His life represents one of the most remarkable stories in the history of the United States.

Born a slave in 1817 on a Talbot County, Maryland, plantation, Douglass, through sheer force of his own character and courage, rose to national prominence and international renown.

As a child he was aided in his self-education by the wife of his master who recognized his promise and taught him to read and write. In 1838, he fled to the free North, riding the Underground Railroad into New England. His new life as a spokesman for Negro rights unfolded by chance one day in August, 1841, when Douglass attended a meeting of white abolitionists in Nantucket, Massachusetts. To his surprise, he was asked to speak—his first speech. Nervous, fumbling for words, he began to tell his story of slavery. People, both black and white, listened and were caught by his intensity.

His brilliance as an orator in the cause of freedom for his people brought him not only fame throughout the North, but the ever-present danger of capture and return to slavery. A lecture tour in England helped the Quakers of that country raise $750 to purchase his freedom.

Returning to the United States in 1847, Douglass settled in Rochester, New York, where for seventeen years he published a newspaper for Negroes, the *North Star.* He later continued his publishing career in Washington, D.C., as editor of the *New National Star,* a weekly for Negroes.

During the Civil War, Douglass recruited thirty thousand troops for the Northern forces. President Lincoln once called him "the most meritorious person I have ever seen."

Douglass supported woman suffrage, narrowly escaped arrest as a conspirator with John Brown, and thundered against slavery as the real cause of the Civil War. He was named to high offices under five presidents and served with distinction. These appointments included Recorder of Deeds, U.S. Marshal for the District of Columbia, and first U.S. Minister to Haiti.

In 1967, the University of Rochester held a Frederick Douglass Sesquicentennial with a series of lectures by prominent Negro scholars and leaders including Benjamin Quarles, professor and chairman, department of history, Morgan State College; John Hope Franklin, professor and chairman, department of history, University of Chicago; Whitney Young, Jr., executive director, National Urban League; Samuel Nabrit, Atomic Energy Commission; Asa T. Spaulding, president, North Carolina Mutual Life Insurance Company; the Honorable William M. Hastie, Third United States Circuit Court of Appeals; John H. Johnson, editor and publisher, *Ebony* Magazine; and Allison Davis, professor, Graduate School of Education, University of Chicago. At the close of the program, the university designated the men's dining center as the Frederick Douglass Building.

Douglass died in Washington on February 20, 1895. Today he is regarded as the father of the civil rights movement.

◆

The first U.S. stamp to honor a Negro musician was that of W. C. Handy, father of the blues. Valued at $.06, it bears a picture of W. C. Handy blowing his horn. It went on sale on May 17, 1969, in Memphis, Tennessee.

State Department

The first Negro official in the U.S. State Department was Dr. Ralph Bunche, who was appointed on January 4, 1944, as Divisional Assistant, Division of Political Studies, Department of State. On July 1, 1946, Bunche went on leave without pay from the Department to work with the United Nations. On March 23, 1947, he was transferred from the State Department to the United Nations.

See also Diplomatic Corps.

State Legislatures

The first Negro representatives to sit in any state legislature were Edwin Garrison Walker and Charles Lewis Mitchell of Boston, Massachusetts, who, in 1866, were elected to the Massachusetts House of Representatives.

◆

The first Negro to serve in the Ohio legislature was John Paterson Greene. He was elected to the Ohio House of Representatives in 1886 and 1888, and to the Ohio State Senate in 1890. It was he who introduced the bill establishing Labor Day, later to become a national holiday.

◆

The first Negro representative to the New Jersey House of Assembly was Walker G. Alexander of Orange, New Jersey, who was elected in 1920. He was also the first to fill the speaker's seat in a Northern state legislature.

◆

The first Negro to be elected to the Missouri state legislature since Reconstruction days was Walthall M. Moore. He was elected on November 5, 1920.

◆

The first Negro woman elected to a state legislature in the United States was Crystal Bird Fauset, acquiring this distinction when she was named to the Pennsylvania House of Representatives on November 8, 1938. She held office for one term. Miss Fauset died on March 28, 1965.

◆

The first Negro to serve in the Alaska legislature was Mrs. Blanche McSmith. She was appointed by Governor William Egan in 1960, after a vacancy occurred when John Radar became the new state's first Attorney General. Mrs. McSmith received her M.A. from the University of Southern California in 1944.

◆

The first Negro state senator in Georgia since Reconstruction was Leroy R. Johnson, who was elected in 1962.

The first Negro woman in the Maryland state senate was Mrs. Verda F. Welcome, who was elected in 1963.

The first foreign-born Negro to serve in the California legislature was Mervyn M. Dymally. He was a leader in the March on Washington in 1963. Dymally was born in Trinidad.

The first Negro state senator in Delaware history was Herman M. Holloway, Sr., who was elected in 1964.

The first Negro to serve in the Connecticut General Assembly was Wilfred X. Johnson from Hartford. He attended the American Institute of Banking.

The first Negro in Oklahoma history to win the Democratic nomination for a legislative seat was John B. White. White was nominated in September, 1964.

The first Negro in Louisiana to win a house seat in the Louisiana legislature since Reconstruction was attorney Ernest Morial of New Orleans. This he won in 1967.

The first Negro member of the Virginia legislature since Reconstruction was Dr. W. Ferguson Reid, a surgeon and a Democrat, who was elected in 1967.

The first Negro member of the Mississippi State legislature since Reconstruction was Robert Clark, schoolteacher and grandson of a slave. He was elected in 1967.

The first black North Carolina lawmaker to serve in this century was Henry E. Frye. He was elected to the North Carolina legislature in 1969.

The first Negro to be elected to the Alabama legislature since Reconstruction was Fred Gray, a black attorney who won by five hundred votes in June, 1970.

The first Negro woman in Louisiana state history to be seated as a member of the Louisiana Legislature was Dorothy Taylor of New Orleans. She took her oath as the first black woman solon May 10, 1971.

Stock Exchange

The first Negro to obtain a seat on the New York Stock Exchange was Joseph L. Searles. The board of governors approved his application in February, 1970.

An honor graduate of Kansas State University, Searles would have had to pay $380,000 for the seat as an individual. However, as a new partner in the brokerage firm of Newberger Loeb & Company, he is taking over a currently inactive seat held by the company.

The board's approval made the thirty-year-old Searles eligible to conduct transactions on the floor of the 178-year-old exchange, which has been referred to as "the second most exclusive club in America," the U.S. Senate being the first.

Sunday Schools

The first Sunday school in the United States, organized in 1786 by Bishop Ashbury of the Methodist Church at the house of David Crenshaw of Maryland, had Negroes among its members. One of the first converts in the school was a Negro, John Charleston, who afterward became a noted preacher. Another celebrated early Negro preacher was known as "Black Harry." This preacher was Bishop Ashbury's traveling companion, and when for any reason the bishop could not fill an appointment, the people were pleased to hear Black Harry.

New York City's first Sunday school was founded by a black woman, Catherine (Katy) Ferguson, in 1793, at her home on Warren Street. Later, Dr. John M. Mason, a prominent minister, made arrangements for her to use the basement of his Murray Street Church. This was the beginning of the Murray Street Sabbath School, which Mrs. Ferguson conducted for more than forty years.

Mrs. Ferguson collected forty-eight children from the poor-house and from destitute parents and raised them or placed them in good homes. Her school was interracial—twenty of her initial brood being white. Emphasis was placed on secular as well as religious education.

Mrs. Ferguson died in 1854. In 1920, in tribute to her and in recognition of her early contributions, the Katy Ferguson Home for unwed mothers was founded in New York.

Supreme Court

See Judges.

Television

The first all-black operated TV station in the U.S. is WOOK-TV, which operates out of Washington, D.C. The UHF station operated by the United Broadcasting Company began operation in 1940, and featured mostly popular music.

The first Negro performer in the United States to have an hour-long "special" on TV was Harry Belafonte, whose first show was broadcast in 1959. One of his two shows won an Emmy award for its excellence. Belafonte was also the first Negro to produce a major show for television. His 1966 *Strollin' Twenties,* with a script by Langston Hughes and Sidney Poitier as narrator, starred Sammy Davis, Jr., Diahann Carroll, and Nipsey Russell.

The first Negro actor to costar in a continuing series (1965) and the first to receive an Emmy (1967) was Bill Cosby. *I Spy,* an hour's thriller series on NBC-TV won national attention for presenting Bill Cosby as costar with Robert Culp.

A native of Philadelphia, Cosby dropped out of high school to become a medic in the navy, obtaining his diploma while in service. On becoming a civilian, he entered Temple University where he played football. He left Temple in 1962, to pursue a career in show business. He began by playing in small clubs around Philadelphia and New York's Greenwich Village. Within two years he was playing top night clubs around the country and making television appearances on such shows as Jack Paar, Johnny Carson, and Andy Williams.

Cosby is the first Negro entertainer to star on network television in a role which has no connection with race.

Tennis

The first Negro tennis player to participate in a U.S. Indoor Lawn Tennis Association championship tournament was Dr. Reginald Weir of New York City, who won his first match on March 11, 1948, and was eliminated from the competition on March 31. The tournament was held in New York City.

◆

The first national tennis tournament of the United States Lawn Tennis Association in which a Negro woman competed was held at the West Side Tennis Club in Forest Hills, New York, in August, 1950. Althea Gibson was the Negro player.

In 1951, Miss Gibson became the first Negro to play at Wimbledon in England. In 1957, she won the Wimbledon singles crown, and teamed with Darlene Hard to win the doubles championship as well. When she returned to New York, she was greeted by a ticker-tape parade in recognition of her position as the best woman tennis player in the world. After a few years in retirement, Althea Gibson returned to tennis in 1970, and has been playing in U.S.L.T.A. tournaments, primarily in doubles competitions.

◆

The first Negro to win the U.S. Amateur Tennis singles championship at Forest Hills was Arthur Ashe in 1968. He is also the first Negro man to win the British singles competition at Wimbledon. He won that title in 1970.

Born in 1943, in Richmond, Virginia, Ashe learned the game at the Richmond Racket Club, which had been formed by local enthusiasts.

In 1961, Ashe entered UCLA on a tennis scholarship. Since then he has beaten most of the world's top players. Tennis great Pancho Gonzales says, "He has the fastest service since mine." Harry Hopman, the coach of the Australian Davis Cup team, regards Ashe as "the most promising player in the world today, and the biggest single threat to our . . . supremacy."

Theater

See Drama.

Towns

The first incorporated town for Negroes in the United States was Eatonville, Florida.

Eatonville received its charter of incorporation in 1883, and the federal writers of Florida said it was the first Negro town with a corporate charter in that state and in the United States. Joe E. Clark was elected mayor in the first election, on August 18, 1886 The *Eatonville Leader* was the first Negro publication in Florida.

Treasury, U.S.

See Money.

United Church of Christ

The first high-ranking Negro executive of the United Church of Christ was the Reverend Joseph H. Evans, who was elected National Secretary of this predominantly white church body in 1967. According to recent reports, membership of Negroes in the United Church is estimated to be around three percent.

Dr. Evans was born in Kalamazoo, Michigan, on August 15, 1915. He received the A.B. degree from Western Michigan

University in 1939, and the B.D. from Yale University in 1942. He was ordained to the ministry of the Congregational Church in 1942. Before coming to the Church of the Good Shepherd in Chicago in 1956, he served at churches in New York City, Hartford, Connecticut, and Cleveland, Ohio. Dr. Evans was pastor of the Chicago church at the time of his election.

United Nations

The first Negro woman appointed to the United Nations was Judge Edith Sampson. She was named in August, 1950, by President Harry S Truman as an Alternate Delegate to the General Assembly. Her membership was renewed in 1952. During that year she was also appointed a member-at-large of the United Nations Educational Scientific and Cultural Organization (UNESCO).

Judge Sampson was born in Pittsburgh, Pennsylvania, on October 13, 1901. She attended the public schools of Pittsburgh. Later, she attended New York's Columbia University School of Social Work, and while there made the highest grade in the required course of criminology. From 1922 to 1925, she studied at the John Marshall Law School in Chicago. She obtained a Bachelor of Law in 1925, and entered the law school of Loyola University. She received a Master of Law in 1927, the first woman to receive that degree from Loyola.

The first Negro to become a permanent member of a U.S. delegation to the United Nations was Charles H. Mahoney, a Detroit lawyer.

Born in Decatur, Michigan, on March 29, 1886, Mahoney received his B.A. from Fisk University, and his LL.B. from the University of Michigan. During his five-year U.N. tour (1954–59), he was an important member of several committees and also served on the Panel of Inquiry and Conciliation. Mahoney died in Detroit on January 26, 1966.

The first Negro to become Undersecretary of the United Nations was Dr. Ralph J. Bunche. In 1955, he was promoted to this post, the highest held by an American Negro in the U.N.

◆

The first Negro with the United States delegation to the U.N. to receive the rank of ambassador was Franklin H. Williams in 1964. He had been with the Peace Corps prior to his appointment.

Unity Churches

The first Negro to head the Association of Unity Churches was the Reverend Johnnie Colemon, minister of Christ Unity Temple in Chicago. She was chosen president of this predominantly white church group at a five-day conference in Lee Summitt, Missouri, on January 20, 1969. Mrs. Colemon, a graduate of Wiley College in Marshall, Texas, has been pastor of Christ Unity Temple since its founding in 1958. Ordained in 1958, she was a member of the board of trustees of the former Unity Minister's Association and for the past three years has been a member of the board of trustees and the executive committee of the Association of Unity Churches. Unity churches are educational centers which aim to give practical application to the teachings of Jesus Christ in daily living. Charles and Myrtle Filmore founded the movement in 1889, in Kansas City, Missouri.

Urban League

The first major national organization concentrating exclusively upon the social and economic problems of Negroes in America's cities was the National Urban League.

Established in 1910, with George E. Haynes as its executive secretary for the first two years and Eugene Kinkle Jones for the next thirty years, the National Urban League, with its local affiliates in over sixty cities, has spearheaded or buttressed gain after gain for the black population.

These gains include better jobs for black workers in a wider spread of occupations; better services for families needing them from public and voluntary welfare agencies; less racial discrimination in public employment offices, hospitals, and schools; and a more intelligent and fairminded handling by public officials of problems involving the rights and needs of black citizens. Currently, the Urban League is broadening its activities to obtain for the Negro and other minority groups a well-rounded community life—better health, housing, school and home conditions, and recreational facilities.

Voting

The first Negro to vote under the authority of the Fifteenth Amendment (March 30, 1870) was Thomas Peterson Mundy of Perth Amboy, New Jersey, who voted on March 31, 1870, in Perth Amboy, in a special election for ratification or rejection of a city charter. The charter was adopted, and he was appointed to the committee to revise the charter.

◆

The first Negroes to vote in Illinois under the authority of the Fifteenth Amendment were David and Charles Strother, who voted at the city elections in El Paso, Illinois, on April 4, 1870. No serious objections were made. They were too late to be registered and voted on affidavit. They were brothers; one voted the Democratic ticket and the other voted the Republican ticket.

Women

The first Negro woman to become an antislavery lecturer was Sojourner Truth. Born as Isabella Baumfree in 1797, in Ulster County, New York, a slave, she is thought to have run away to freedom and worked as a domestic.

In 1843, she felt an overpowering urge to speak out against slavery. Already deeply religious, she suddenly felt reborn, in the spring of that year. In her own words, she declared, "I felt tall within as if the power of the nation was with me." Isabella then renamed herself Sojourner Truth and assumed as her mission in life the task of traveling across the country and spreading "the truth." She thundered against slavery and for women's suffrage on countless rostrums, secure in the knowledge that she was a chosen vessel of the Lord. Though illiterate, she had the reputation of an oracle.

Even after the Civil War was over, Sojourner Truth continued traveling up and down the country on behalf of her people, campaigning in particular for better educational opportunities. Her *Narrative,* published in 1875, recounts her entire life, notably including her war experiences, as well as a meeting with Abraham Lincoln. She died in Michigan on November 26, 1883.

The first and greatest Negro conductor on the Underground Railroad—an organized network of way-stations which helped Negro slaves escape from the South to the free states and as far North as Canada—was a woman named Harriet Ross Tubman who was a former slave.

She was born in about 1820, in Dorchester County, Maryland. In 1848, she escaped from her master and went to New York. In her own words, she described her first taste of liberty: "I was free and I couldn't believe it. There was such a glory all around and the sun was shining through the trees and on the hills. I was free!"

Once free she began to devise practical ways to help other slaves escape. Over the next ten years, she made some twenty trips from the North to the South, bringing more than three hundred slaves to freedom and eventually having a price of $40,000 set on her head. But Harriet, who had great faith in God, led a seemingly charmed life. She always outwitted her pursuers.

During the Civil War, Harriet served the Union cause openly and actively as nurse, soldier, spy, and scout. She was particularly valuable in this latter capacity, since her work on the railroad had made her thoroughly familiar with much of the terrain.

After the war, Harriet settled in Auburn, New York. She applied for a military pension, but it was thirty years before she received it. When it was granted, she used the money to found a home for the aged.

She died in Auburn in 1913, and was buried in Ohio with military honors.

The first Negro woman in the country to hold a position on a school board was Mary Church Terrell, who was appointed by the commissioners of Washington, D.C., to this position in 1895. Ironing out disputes between teachers and principals and soothing angry parents, she also did her utmost to improve the quality of the education that the children received.

Mary Church Terrell was born in 1863 and died in 1954.

When the National Association of Colored Women was organized in 1896, she was its first president, and thereafter elected honorary president for life. She continued making contributions to clubwork and to the advancement of blacks in America. In 1933, Oberlin College included Mrs. Terrell among its one hundred outstanding graduates, and in 1948, her alma mater bestowed upon her the doctorate of humane letters. During 1940, she earned the distinction of being named by Oberlin College as one of the one hundred American women who had made singular and outstanding contributions during the last century.

◆

The first known Negro woman to become an aviatrix was twenty-four-year-old Betty Coleman of Chicago. She attended an aviation school in France and returned home as a full-fledged aviatrix in 1920.

◆

The first Negro delegate to the International Council of Women, held in Norway in 1920, was Mary B. Talbert. She was also the first woman to receive the Spingarn Medal in 1922.

◆

The first Negro woman to win the Spingarn Medal was Mary B. Talbert, former president of the National Association of Colored Women. It was awarded on June 20, 1922, in Newark, New Jersey, for services to the women of her race and for the restoration of the home of Frederick Douglass. Miss Talbert was a graduate of Oberlin College, and was considered one of the foremost speakers of her race.

◆

The first Negro woman to become Mother of the Year was Mrs. Emma Clement—the mother of an illustrious family, which includes Dr. Rufus Clement, president of Atlanta University, and

Mrs. Abbie Clement Jackson, outstanding churchwoman. Mrs. Clement received this honor in 1946.

The first woman and the first Negro to serve as an Assistant Secretary of State was Barbara Watson. She was appointed in 1967, and attributed this honor to President Lyndon B. Johnson's recognition that no nation can progress "without the skills and abilities of all its citizens." She credits Johnson with doing more than any of his predecessors to "use the abilities of women in government."

Her consular domain includes 280 posts throughout the world ranging from large embassies in London and Paris to small consulates serving countries some Americans have never heard of. In Washington, a large percentage of her six hundred employees distribute passports to Americans going abroad.

It is the traveling Americans who present Miss Watson with most of the problems that plague the "crisis bureau. Our special services office," she explained, "is charged with the full-time responsibility for protecting American citizens in other countries whether they become sick and die, get into jail or become pawns of war."

The first Negro female colonel in the Army Nurse Corps was Margaret E. Bailey, who was promoted to this rank in February, 1970. Colonel Bailey is presently assigned to the U.S. Army Element, Job Corps Health Office in the Department of Labor.

The first Negro woman to be awarded the Constance Lindsay Skinner Award of the Women's National Book Association was Charlmae Hill Rollins. This most coveted award in the professional book world was presented to Mrs. Rollins at a banquet in her honor at the Walnut Room of the Bismark Hotel in Chicago, on April 10, 1970.

Mrs. Rollins for many years was the director of children's activities at the George Cleveland Hall Library of the Chicago Public Library. She has also taught numerous classes in children's literature at Roosevelt University, Rosary College, and at seminars and institutes in colleges and universities across the nation.

The bibliography, "We Build Together," published in the late 1940's by the National Council of Teachers of English was first completed under Mrs. Rollins' direction. In "We Build Together," books for children were examined with an eye to their portrayal of black characters, and recommendations were made accordingly.

Mrs. Rollins is the author of *Christmas Gift, They Showed the Way, Famous Negro Poets,* and *Famous Negroes of Stage, Screen and TV.* She has also completed a biography of Langston Hughes.

The first woman to receive an appointment as apprentice printer in the Bureau of Engraving and Printing was Mrs. Virginia Spann Gould, a Negro. She received her appointment in March, 1971.

In her new position, which is one of the highest paying jobs in the Bureau, Mrs. Gould will be printing all denominations of currency, stamps, U.S. bonds, and Treasury notes.

She was one of 350 applicants to take the Civil Service examination for the position and was awarded the printer apprenticeship after receiving the highest score on the examination.

The first black woman president of Church Women United was Clarie Collins Harvey of Jackson, Mississippi. She was elected at its triennial Ecumenical Assembly meeting in May, 1971.

In 1961 Mrs. Harvey founded Woman-power Unlimited, an interracial human relations group of Protestant, Jewish, and Catholic women who provided housing, prison ministries, and aid to the civil rights advocates coming into Mississippi. Since 1964 she has been a member of the Mississippi Advisory Committee to the United States Commission on Civil Rights.

Church Women United is a national movement offering Protestant, Roman Catholic, and Orthodox women an opportunity to express their faith through work. The national movement has branches in every state.

The first Negro woman in the United Nations.

See United Nations.

The first Negro woman ambassador.

See Ambassadors.

The first Negro woman to earn a B.A. degree.

See Education.

The first Negro woman Colonel.

See Armed Forces.

The first Negro woman M.D.

See Medicine.

The first Negro woman to be awarded an honorary doctorate from a white college in the South.

See Education.

The first Negro woman judge in the U.S.

See Judges.

The first Negro woman legislator in the U.S.

See State Legislatures.

The first Negro woman to serve as postmistress.

See Post Office.

The first Negro woman to earn a Ph.D.

See Education.

The first Negro woman to write poetry in America.

See Literature.

The first Negro woman to publish a novel.

See Literature.

The first Negro woman to be seated as a member of the Louisiana state legislature.

See State Legislatures.

The first Negro Pulitzer Prize winner.

See Literature.

The first Negro woman to be elected president of the national YWCA.

See YWCA.

Writing

See Literature.

YMCA

The first Negro Young Men's Christian Association was founded in the year 1853 in Washington, D.C., by Anthony Bowen and Jerome Johnson, who served respectively as president and secretary; the second was founded in Charleston, South Carolina, in 1866; and the third in New York City, in 1867.

The first YMCA student organization in a Negro institution was established at Howard University in 1869.

The first money ever contributed toward a fund for a Negro YMCA building, according to the organization's records, was the sum of $10 at Winsboro, South Carolina.

The first salaried employee of the Negro race to serve in the work of the YMCA among Negroes was William A. Hunton, who received $800 a year for his services from the Norfolk, Virginia, YMCA, in January, 1888. So faithful, patient, and efficient was he in his work that it was decided by the International Committee in 1890 to employ him as International Secretary for Negro work throughout the country. He remained in this office until his death on November 27, 1916.

The first black man to be chosen head of the national council of the Young Men's Christian Association in its 125-year history was Donald M. Payne, of Newark, New Jersey. Payne was 35 at the time of his election in 1970. Since he was nominated without opposition of the YMCA's annual convention in Pittsburgh, attended by five hundred delegates, he was elected formally and installed as council president of the convention's closing session. Payne, a widower with children, is employed by the Prudential Insurance Company in Newark as a community relations expert. He has been active in YMCA work since 1937.

YWCA

The first Negro woman to be elected president of the National Young Women's Christian Association was Mrs. Robert Clayton of Grand Rapids, Michigan, who was named to a three-year term at the closing session of the organization's twenty-fourth national convention in Boston, Massachusetts, on April 29, 1967.

As president of the Grand Rapids YWCA from 1949 to 1951, Mrs. Clayton was the first Negro to serve as president of the city YWCA. She has been a national board member since 1945, has served as vice-president-at-large, and represented the YWCA of the United States at the World YWCA Council in Geneva, Switzerland.

A graduate of the University of Minnesota, Mrs. Clayton is on the advisory committee of the Michigan Welfare League and the Michigan Youth Committee, and serves on the boards of other state and local organizations.

◆

The first black executive director of the YWCA of metropolitan Chicago was Miss Doris V. Wilson, who was elected to this important post on September 1, 1969.

Miss Wilson has had extensive experience with the YWCA. She served on the Rocky Mountain and Southern field staffs of the National YWCA Board. She was executive director of the University YWCA serving the UCLA campus, and she joined the Chicago YWCA as director of the first YWCA human relations department in the United States.

INDEX

DATE DUE

NO 20 '78			
FE 25 '79			
MR 15 '79			
JY 9 '80			
MR 23 '82			
GAYLORD			PRINTED IN U.S.A.